Foreword

Welcome to America's Army! You have taken the first step on a journey that I'm confident will change your life forever. Upon completion of your Basic Combat training you will earn the title "Soldier" and with continued honorable service you will always be a "Soldier for Life".

The Army you are joining is a time honored Profession that's the best in the world at what it does. It's comprised of magnificent Soldiers and Civilians who are out there every day making a difference in a very complex world.

The Army Values of loyalty, duty, respect, selfless service, honor, integrity, and personal courage are more than mere words that we recite. Taken together and integrated through an understanding and appreciation of the sacrifices made by the generations of Citizen-Soldiers who previously answered the call to defend America's freedoms...those shared values and beliefs become your moral and ethical identity as Soldiers and Trusted Army Professionals."

Over the next several weeks, we will help you transition from a citizen volunteer to become a Trusted Army Professional, by developing your character, competence, commitment and teaching you what it means to be a Soldier who is physically and mentally ready to accomplish any assigned mission." I'm confident that you are up to the task. I hope you will find this experience personally and professionally rewarding, and, if you let it, it will set you on a path of continued success. So, let's get started!

Anthony C. Funkhouser
Major General, U.S. Army
Commander, Center for Initial Military Training

Soldier Information

Name: _____

My Basic Combat Training (BCT)/One Station Unit Training (OSUT)/Advanced Individual Training (AIT) Company Chain of Command:

* Note: Use pencil

Company Commander: _____

First Sergeant: _____

Drill Sergeant/AITPSG _____

Drill Sergeant/AITPSG _____

Drill Sergeant/AITPSG _____

Instructor / Squad Leader: _____

Instructor / Squad Leader: _____

My mailing address:

_____
_____
_____
_____

My Battle Buddy is...

_____

My Sexual Harassment/Assault Response & Prevention (SHARP) Program Contacts:
Fill in using a pencil upon arrival at BCT, AIT and/or OSUT, and first unit of assignment:

Unit Victim's Advocate / SHARP Representatives:

Company: _____

Battalion: _____

Brigade: _____

Notes: _____

_____

_____

_____

_____

Basic Combat Training (BCT) Calendar
This is a tool for you to record milestones (APFT, rifle marksmanship, FTX, etc.) and to count down the days until BCT Graduation.

BCT Calendar	Monday	Tuesday	Wednesday
Week 1			
Week 2			
Week 3			
Week 4			
Week 5			
Week 6			
Week 7			
Week 8			
Week 9			
Week 10			

Thursday	Friday	Saturday	Sunday

Notes:

Department of the Army *TRADOC Pamphlet 600-4
Headquarters, United States Army
Training and Doctrine Command
Fort Eustis, VA 23604-5701

23 June 2017

The Soldier's Blue Book

FOR THE COMMANDER:

OFFICIAL: SEAN B. MacFARLAND
Lieutenant General, U.S. Army
Deputy Commanding General/
Chief of Staff

RICHARD A. DAVIS
Senior Executive
Deputy Chief of Staff, G-6

History. This is a rapid action revision to United States Army Training and Doctrine Command Pamphlet 600-4. The portions affected by this revision are listed in the Summary of Change.

*This pamphlet supersedes TRADOC Pamphlet 600-4, dated 18 Jul 2016.

Summary. This pamphlet is the guide for all Initial Entry Training (IET) Soldiers who enter our Army Profession. It provides an introduction to being a Soldier and Trusted Army Professional, certified in character, competence, and commitment to the Army. Throughout the Blue Book, Soldiers will read and learn about Army ethics and our Values, Culture, History, Organizations, and Training they will receive. It provides assistance with pay issues, leave, Thrift Saving Plans (TSPs), and organizations that will be available to assist Families. The Soldier's Blue Book is an inspectable item and will be carried at all times during BCT/OSUT, and AIT.

Applicability. This pamphlet applies to all active Army, United States Army Reserve, and the Army National Guard enlisted IET conducted at service schools, Army Training Centers, and other training activities under the control of Headquarters Training and Doctrine Command (TRADOC).

Proponent. The proponent for this pamphlet is TRADOC Commanding General United States Army Center for Initial Military Training (USACIMT) (ATMT-OP), (ATTN: Jim Rose) 210 Dillon Circle, Fort Eustis VA 23604-5701.

Supplementation. Users are invited to send comments and suggested improvements on Department of the Army (DA) Form 2028 (recommended Changes to Publications and Blank Forms) directly to the U.S. Army Center for Initial

Military Training (ATMT-OP), 210 Dillon Circle, Fort Eustis, VA 23604-5701.

Distribution. This pamphlet will be distributed to the four training locations that conduct BCT and OSUT. This pamphlet is available electronically only on the TRADOC Homepage at http://www.tradoc.army.mil/tpubs.

Summary of Change

TRADOC Pamphlet 600-4
The Soldier's Blue Book

This rapid action revision, dated 23 June 2017-

o Changes cover Picture
o Modifies the graduation requirements in Basic Combat Training and One Station Unit Training (chap 4)
o Modifies paragraph 8-1 Nutrition
o Adds "Manual of Applied Performance Skills (MAPS)" as Appendix B.

This page intentionally left blank

Table of Contents
Page

Foreword i
Soldier Information ii
My Battle Buddy is… iii
My Sexual Harassment/Assault Response & Prevention (SHARP) Program Contacts iii
Basic Combat Training (BCT) Calendar iii
Introduction 9
Chapter 1 – The Army 12
1-1. Why we have an Army 13
1-2. What the Army uniform represents 16
1-3. Why we serve 17
1-4. The Army's Motto – "This We'll Defend" 18
1-5. Oath of Enlistment 19
Chapter 2 – The Army as a Profession 21
2-1. The Army Profession 21
2-2 What it means to be a Soldier 23
2-3. Who we are not 23
2-4. The Army's commitment to you 24
2-5. The journey begins 26
Chapter 3 – The Reception Battalion 27
3-1. The Path 27
3-2. Critical information needed upfront 30
3-3. The Battle Buddy System 30
3-4. Army Values 32
3-5. Suicide Prevention 35
3-6. The Soldier's Creed and Warrior Ethos 36

Chapter 4 – BCT / OSUT / AIT 40
4-1. What to expect 40
4-2. The training company – Your unit 40
4-3. Safe and Secure Environment 42
4-4. Drill Sergeants 43
4-5. The Soldierization process 48
4-6. Military time 49
4-7. Daily schedule 50
4-8. Basic Combat Training (BCT) 50
4-9. Warrior Tasks and Battle Drills 52
4-10. BCT graduation requirements 54
4-11. AIT/OSUT 56
4-12. What is the difference between Drill Sergeants and AIT Platoon Sergeants? 58
Chapter 5 – Personal Appearance and Uniforms 63
5-1. Personal appearance 63
5-2. Army Combat Uniform (ACU) 72
5-3. Army Service Uniform (ASU) 78
5-4. Awards and Decorations 86
Chapter 6 – Critical Information Required for BCT / OSUT / AIT 88
6-1. Rank Insignia 88
6-2. Customs and Courtesies 94
6-3. Bugle Calls 101
6-4. Drill and Ceremonies 102
Chapter 7 – Physical Readiness 107
7-1. Army Physical Fitness Uniform (APFU) 107
7-2. Army physical fitness test (APFT) 109
7-3. APFT Standards 110

Chapter 8 – Health and Safety 114
8-1. Nutrition... 114
8-2. Sleep 122
8-3. Activity... 124
8-4. Hygiene 126
8-5. Ready and Resilient.. 141
8-6. Chaplains 143
8-7. Risk management 143
Chapter 9 – Discipline...145
9-1. Uniform Code of Military Justice (UCMJ)............. 146
9-2. Equal opportunity policy.. 149
9-3. Policy on relationships between Soldiers 152
9-4. SHARP 158
9-5. The Army Ethic 170
9-6. Standards and Principles of Ethical Conduct 175
Chapter 10 – Reference Material 178
10-1. The National Anthem 178
10-2. The Army Song 179
10-3. The Code of Conduct.. 180
10-4. General Orders/Special Orders 182
10-5. Guard duty 183
10-6. Army Organizations 185
Chapter 11 – First Duty Station 186
11-1. Where Will I Serve? 186
11-2. How can I prepare?... 187
11-3. Promotions 187
11-4. Total Army Sponsorship Program (TASP) and Army Career Tracker (ACT) 191
11-5. Soldier for Life Program 194

Appendix A – Army Resources 195
A-1. Leave and Earnings Statement 195
A-2. Managing personal finances 198
A-3. Tri-Service Health Care (TRICARE) 204
A-4. Servicemembers' Group Life Insurance (SGLI) . 205
A-5. Dental 206
A-6. Army Emergency Relief 207
A-7. Soldier for Life and Credentialing 211
A-8. Information websites for family members 215
Appendix B – Manual of Applied Performance Skills (MAPS) 219
Appendix C – Soldier's Notes 267
Glossary 273
Army Definitions 274

The "Blue Book"

Introduction

Since 1775, the United States Army has exhibited unwavering courage, self-discipline, and advanced military training. Soldiers, like you, have volunteered to serve and fight to protect their Families and friends from enemies that sought to do us harm, and to defend the ideals of our nation. Starting from humble beginnings in our quest for freedom, we have become the most powerful Army in the world.

We are an Army made up of individuals, and the strength of each one of us contributes to the strength of the whole. We gain strength from training, and the basis for our training stems from a past deeply rooted in determination and adaptability.

From the formation of the Continental Army in 1775 until Valley Forge, American forces were brave and fought with purpose, but were disorganized citizens fighting against highly trained and better organized British Soldiers. To win the Revolutionary War, General George Washington's men needed enhanced training, discipline, and esprit de corps.

Seeking a solution, General Washington tasked Baron von Steuben with transforming the large group of hungry and exhausted men at Valley Forge into a disciplined fighting force. In the harsh Pennsylvania winter, Baron von Steuben instructed a company of future leaders in basic military movements and tactical skills; those individuals were the predecessors of our Drill Sergeants!

He developed that cadre until they could–in turn–train the entire Revolutionary Army in the art of basic military maneuvers. Through their perseverance and sense of duty, these dedicated troops practiced to the highest standards. As a result, Washington's men fought skillfully in battle afterwards and it was at that time they embodied the principles and discipline that distinguished them as a professional army.

Their perseverance, commitment to the cause, and disciplined execution of their military tasks enabled America to win its independence from England in 1783.

Training to standard and gaining the inner strength to adapt and overcome adversity became the theme for our Army's training model. Baron von Steuben, by then the Army Inspector General, wrote the *Regulations for the Order and Discipline of the Troops of the United States*—now commonly referred to as the Blue Book—an instructional guide for future generations. This book consists, as our modern version does now, of detailed training procedures, the standards of military conduct, and the fundamentals every Soldier needs to know to succeed.

Use this version of the "Blue Book" on the journey on which you are about to undertake. Just as Soldiers before you trained to serve and protect our Nation, this book will help you to learn, train and perform the tasks required of you to become Soldiers in the United States Army.

Chapter 1 – The Army

On 14 June 1775, the Second Continental Congress established "the American Continental Army." The United States Army is the senior Service of the Armed Forces. As one of the oldest American institutions, it predates the Declaration of Independence and the Constitution. For almost two and a half centuries, Army forces have protected this Nation. Our Army flag is adorned with over 190 campaign and battle streamers to date, each one signifying great sacrifices on behalf of the Nation.

Because of the Army, the United States is independent and one undivided nation.

1-1. Why we have an Army

It is the intent of Congress to provide an Army that is capable, in conjunction with the other armed forces, of...

Preserving the peace and security, and providing for the defense of the United States, the Commonwealths and possessions, and any areas occupied by the United States;

Supporting the national policies;

Implementing the national objectives; and

Overcoming any nations responsible for aggressive acts that imperil the peace and security of the United States.

Title 10, U.S. Code, Section 3062(a)

TIMELINE OF THE U.S. ARMY

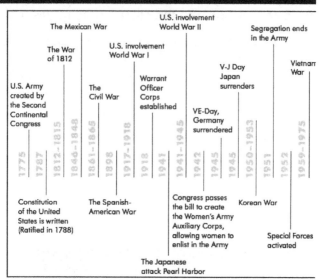

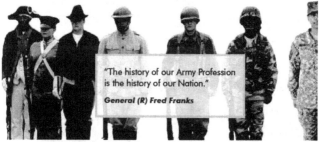

"The history of our Army Profession is the history of our Nation."

General (R) Fred Franks

1775 to Present

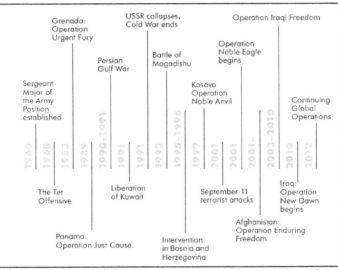

TRADOC Pamphlet 600-4

1-2. What the Army uniform represents

For Soldiers it means that they are part of something far bigger than themselves...it is an opportunity to serve this great country and to make a difference in this world.

For Army Families, the uniform is a source of both pride and sacrifice.

Living by and upholding the Army Ethics is our life-long commitment. For our veterans, it represents one of the most important periods of their lives...pride in honorable service, accomplishments as part of a team, and a life-long connection to the comrades with whom they served, and in some cases, lost during their time in uniform.

When Soldiers return to society as private citizens, they are expected to continue to be moral-ethical role models for their Families and communities, contributing to the well-being of the United States of America, as Soldiers for Life.

For the American citizen, Soldiers are their sons, daughters, relatives, neighbors, and during disaster, their lifeline. In us they see patriotism and selfless service, and heroism. Being seen as heroes you are expected to uphold a higher standard and represent yourself and community as a source of pride and commitment.

People around the world recognize the American Soldier as a symbol of the United States...Soldiers represent freedom, democracy, and stability.

To our enemies, the Soldier represents American strength, resolve, and a commitment to defend the values that we hold dear as a Nation.

1-3. Why we serve

As Soldiers, we are committed to do our duty to contribute to the "common defense;" we share a love of our country and of our Army Family; we defend American values that frame the nation as expressed in the Declaration of Independence and the Constitution of the United States; and we serve "not to promote war, but to preserve peace."

1-4. The Army's Motto – "This We'll Defend"

The Army's motto remains as relevant today as it did at our Nation's founding. The pronoun "We" reinforces our collective or team effort and "Defend" remains our Army's main mission. The Army continues this pledge into the future, as we have done since 1775.

Department of the Army Emblem

1-5. Oath of Enlistment

> **ARMY OATH OF ENLISTMENT**
>
> "I, _____, do solemnly swear (or affirm) that I will support and defend the Constitution of the United States against all enemies, foreign and domestic; that I will bear true faith and allegiance to the same; and that I will obey the orders of the President of the United States and the orders of the officers appointed over me, according to regulations and the Uniform Code of Military Justice. So help me God." (Title 10, US Code; Act of 5 May 1960).

Members of the American military profession swear or affirm to support and defend the Constitution of the United States—not a leader, people, government, or territory.

That solemn oath ties service in the Army directly to the founding document of the United States. It instills a nobility of purpose within each member of the Army Profession and provides deep personal meaning to all who serve.

The Army Profession believes America must have a Professional Army of Soldiers and Civilians who are inspired to honorably fulfill their Oaths of Service. We accomplish our missions as a team, partnering with the other armed forces in the joint community and with government services that dedicate themselves to defending the U.S. Constitution and protect the Nation's interests, at home and abroad, against all threats."

Chapter 2 – The Army as a Profession

2-1. The Army Profession

Our identity, as trusted Army professionals, derives from our shared understanding of and respect for those whose legacy we celebrate. We honor this cherished inheritance in our customs, courtesies, and traditions. Units and organizations preserve their storied histories and proudly display distinctive emblems (regimental colors, crests, insignia, patches, and mottos). The campaign streamers on the Army flag remind us of our history of honorable service to the Nation. These symbols recall the sacrifices and preserve the ties with those who preceded us.

Our Army Profession has two mutually supporting communities of practice—

- *The Profession of Arms*, Soldiers of the Regular Army, Army National Guard, and Army Reserve.
- *The Army Civilian Corps*, composed of civilian professionals serving in the Department of the Army.

Profession of Arms: Uniformed members of the Army Profession—Soldiers. This includes the Regular Army, Army National Guard, and Army Reserve.

The Army Ethic: An evolving set of laws, values, and beliefs, deeply embedded within the core of the Army culture and practiced by all members of the Army Profession to motivate and guide the appropriate conduct of individual members bound together in common moral purpose.

"A soldier is the most-trusted profession in America. Americans have trust in you because you trust each other".

9th Sergeant Major of the Army Richard A. Kidd

2-2 What it means to be a Soldier

The Army is an honored profession, founded on a bedrock of Trust – trust between Soldiers; trust between Soldiers and Leaders; Trust between Soldiers and Army Civilians; trust between Solders, their Families and the Army; and trust between the Army and the American people. By our solemn oath, we are morally committed to support and defend the Constitution. This duty requires a foundation of trust with the American people who grant us autonomy to use lethal force on their behalf, only because we have earned their trust. Army professionals understand and accept that they may give their lives and justly take the lives of others to accomplish the mission. The moral implications of this realization compel essential bonds of mutual trust within cohesive teams. The Nation tasks the Army to do many things besides combat operations, but ultimately, the primary reason the Army exists is to fight and win our Nation's wars through prompt and sustained land combat as part of the joint force. The Army and each of its members must maintain the readiness to accomplish this mission, now and in the future. Once a Soldier, always a Soldier…A Soldier for Life.

2-3. Who we are not

Army Professionals do not engage in or tolerate acts of misconduct or unethical decisions. Actions such as sexual harassment, sexual assault, and hazing are dishonorable and contrary to the Army Values and the

Army's Professional Ethos and destroy esprit de corps. One incident is one too many.

Sexual Harassment is a form of gender discrimination that involves unwelcome sexual advances, requests for sexual favors, and other verbal or physical conduct of a sexual nature.

Sexual Assault is a CRIME and can result in a felony offense. Sexual assault is defined as intentional sexual contact, characterized by use of force, threats, intimidation or abuse of authority, or when the victim does not or cannot consent. Sexual assault includes rape, forcible sodomy and other unwanted sexual contact that is aggravated, abusive, or wrongful or attempts to commit these acts. This includes touching of the breasts, buttocks, genitalia or any other part of the body to satisfy sexual desires. *During training, there is no such thing as a consensual relationship.*

Hazing is defined as any conduct whereby one military member or employee, regardless of Service or rank, unnecessarily causes another military member or employee, regardless of Service or rank, to suffer or be exposed to an activity that is cruel, abusive, or harmful.

2-4. The Army's commitment to you
Our commitment to you is to help guide you on this journey from an aspiring member of the Army Profession to a Soldier.

We are committed to providing you with a safe and secure environment where everyone can live, train, and learn, while developing into Soldiers of...

- ➢ Character: Soldiers who understand, adhere to, and uphold the Army Ethic, as demonstrated by their decisions and actions.

- ➢ Competence: Soldiers who demonstrate the ability to perform basic combat skills and who demonstrate entry-level proficiency in their designated occupational specialty.

- ➢ Commitment: Soldiers who understand the calling to honorable service and sacrifice, in the defense of our Nation, who perform their duties successfully with discipline and to standard, and who successfully and ethically accomplish the mission despite adversity, obstacles, and challenges.

In turn, you join the ranks of generations of Soldiers who previously answered the call to defend America's freedoms; you join a band of brothers and sisters who are prepared to serve this Nation in peace and in war; and join the Profession of Arms, a profession dedicated to upholding the values and ideals of our Country and its people that we serve and represent.

Our desired outcome as you complete your initial certification process is to provide the Army with a Soldier...

- Who has internalized the Army Ethic, accepting the calling to the shared identity of being a Trusted Army Professional, as demonstrated by your decisions and actions.

- Who is agile, adaptive and resilient.

- Who is physically ready to execute required Soldier and occupational specialty skills.

- Who is ready to serve as a trusted member of a team in their first unit of assignment.

2-5. The journey begins

When you took the Oath of Enlistment, you became a member of the Army Profession, albeit an aspiring professional or apprentice.

The task at hand is to develop and certify you in the Army Profession of Character, Competence and Commitment. The responsibility for each individual's development and certification is a mutual one, a trusted bond, shared between you, your leaders, and the Army.

The first certification in becoming an Army Professional is the most critical one. This involves providing you with the knowledge and skills to serve as a practicing professional in your first unit of assignment.

Chapter 3 – The Reception Battalion

3-1. The Path

Welcome to the Reception Battalion. By being here, this means that you have met your initial entry qualification requirements. While at the Military Entrance Processing Station you underwent a battery of aptitude tests and medical examinations to determine if you were qualified for military service. Congratulations, you passed!

You've been vetted mentally, physically, and intellectually, by passing the Occupational Physical Assessment Test (OPAT), and the Armed Services Vocational Aptitude Battery (ASVAB). You know what your future military occupational specialty (MOS/Job) will be, and are sworn into the United States Army. Now it's time for you to begin the transformation to becoming a Soldier.

You are at one of the following **Basic Combat Training/ One Station Unit Training** locations:

- Fort Benning, Georgia
- Fort Jackson, South Carolina
- Fort Leonard Wood, Missouri
- Fort Sill, Oklahoma

If your MOS is 11B/11C (Infantryman), 19D (Cavalry Scout), 19K (Armor Crewman), 12B (Combat Engineer) or 31B (Military Police Officer), you will conduct your Basic Combat Training and occupational skills training in one course. This is called "One Station Unit Training" or "OSUT" and is conducted at Fort Benning for 11B and 19K Soldiers, and at Fort Leonard Wood for 12B and 31B Soldiers.

All other Soldiers will go through "Basic Combat Training" or "BCT" at one of the four locations listed above, and upon completion, will attend a follow-on course called "Advanced Individual Training" or "AIT." This course may be at the same installation as your BCT training or may be at another location.

While at the Reception Battalion, you will undergo further medical and dental processing. Medical and dental processing will include collection of blood for certain immunities, type, and DNA; hearing and vision exams (in addition to the MEPS exams); pregnancy screening; tuberculosis screening; immunizations; and a brief dental exam and x-rays. You will receive ear plugs, eyewear and eye protection, and personal protective items such as sunscreen. These are all items of "individual medical readiness" that you will maintain throughout your career.

You will also undergo further administrative processing (personnel and finance records, and security clearance if applicable).

You will receive a standard military haircut, be issued your initial clothing requirement, to include physical fitness and Army Combat Uniforms (ACUs), footwear and miscellaneous clothing items. You will be taught how to properly wear the clothing issued and begin to learn the basics of military culture.

Your actions and ability to follow instructions will be monitored carefully. A Drill Sergeant or cadre member will take you through the stations required for you to enter into the Army.

Follow all instructions and pay attention to detail. One of the key elements to being successful in the Army is ensuring you understand what is required of you and ask questions if you are unsure.

A typical stay in the Reception Battalion lasts from 3-5 days for BCT Soldiers and 5-7 days for OSUT Soldiers.

When you complete reception in-processing, you will be assigned to a training company. Drill Sergeants will pick you up at the Reception Battalion and travel with you to your BCT or OSUT company location.

Eagle Cash Stored Value Card: While at the Reception Battalion, you will be issued a Stored Value Card. The stored value card reduces cash/check operations for the initial trainee advance. The card can be used at the Army and Air Force Exchange Service (AAFES) sites (barber shops, clothing sales, and Post Exchange facilities).

Any remaining value at expiration is returned to the Soldier; however, spending the full amount prior to completion of training is encouraged. Advance amount on the Eagle Cash Card is $350. The Value Card will expire 45 days from initial issue to Soldiers at the Reception Battalion.

3-2. Critical information needed upfront

During your stay at the Reception Battalion, BCT or OSUT, you will be expected to read, study, and memorize all necessary information. The purpose of the information is to introduce and reinforce who we are as Army Professionals and what we represent as Soldiers. Your job is to fully understand, comprehend and demonstrate your proficiency by reciting it to the Drill Sergeant and leaders either individually or as a group.

Information identified by a "star" requires comprehension by memorization.

3-3. The Battle Buddy System

Soldiers rely on one another to stay motivated and reach peak performance. Although required in Initial Military Training, Soldiers will form natural bonds with their fellow Soldiers as part of Army culture. To contribute to this team spirit, we live by the buddy system. A buddy team is usually defined as two Soldiers in the same unit who look after each other at all times.

By getting to know other Soldiers on a professional and personal level, you learn how to improve yourself and encourage others. Working together, you and your battle buddy learn initiative, responsibility, trust, and dependability.

While at the Reception Battalion, BCT, OSUT and AIT, same-gender Soldiers (male-male and female-female) are placed in buddy teams. With the requirement to excel in Army training, some Soldiers need more positive reinforcement than others. For that reason, you may also be paired based on your strengths, so you and your buddy can complement each other's weaknesses.

Battle Buddy responsibilities:

- Never leave your buddy alone
- Never let your buddy go into an office or room by themselves; even if a Drill Sergeant, Platoon Sergeant or Instructor says it's okay
- Keep your buddy safe and free from harm
- Know the whereabouts of your buddy at all times
- Pass information to your buddy
- Encourage and support your buddy to train harder and do better
- Help your buddy solve problems
- Inform Cadre of any changes in your buddy's behavior

In the end, the most rewarding part of the buddy system is making _every_ Soldier your buddy; for any one of them could help you accomplish your mission or save your life in combat.

3-4. Army Values

Our ethical and moral foundation as Soldiers are solidified in the seven Army Values—

Loyalty, Duty, Respect, Selfless Service, Honor, Integrity, and Personal Courage.

They are at the core of who we are as individuals, as Soldiers, as Professionals and as Americans. Whether on or off-duty, Soldiers live these values every day.

The easiest way to remember the Army Values is through the acronym "**LDRSHIP**".

LOYALTY: Bear true faith and allegiance to the U.S. Constitution, the Army, your unit, and other Soldiers.

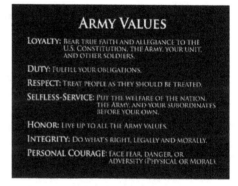

ARMY VALUES

LOYALTY: BEAR TRUE FAITH AND ALLEGIANCE TO THE U.S. CONSTITUTION, THE ARMY, YOUR UNIT, AND OTHER SOLDIERS.
DUTY: FULFILL YOUR OBLIGATIONS.
RESPECT: TREAT PEOPLE AS THEY SHOULD BE TREATED.
SELFLESS-SERVICE: PUT THE WELFARE OF THE NATION, THE ARMY, AND YOUR SUBORDINATES BEFORE YOUR OWN.
HONOR: LIVE UP TO ALL THE ARMY VALUES.
INTEGRITY: DO WHAT'S RIGHT, LEGALLY AND MORALLY.
PERSONAL COURAGE: FACE FEAR, DANGER, OR ADVERSITY (PHYSICAL OR MORAL).

Bearing true faith and allegiance is a matter of believing in and dedicating yourself to the United States of America and the U.S. Army. A loyal Soldier is one who supports his or her leader and stands up for fellow Soldiers. By wearing the uniform of the U.S. Army you are expressing your loyalty to the Nation, Family, and your fellow Soldiers.

DUTY: Fulfill your obligations.

Doing your duty means carrying out your assigned tasks and being able to accomplish the mission as part of a team. Duty also requires you to work hard every day to be a better Soldier. Everyone in our Army contributes to the mission if they do their duty.

RESPECT: Treat people as you yourself would want to be treated.

Respect allows us to appreciate the best in other people. Respect is trusting that all people have done their jobs and fulfilled their duty. Self-respect is also a vital ingredient and is a result from knowing you have put forth your best effort. The Army is one team, and all contribute best when they are treated with respect.

SELFLESS SERVICE: Put the welfare of the Nation, the Army, and your subordinates before your own.

In serving your country, you are doing your duty loyally without thought of recognition, reward, or personal comfort. Selfless services is the commitment of each team member to go a little further, endure a little longer, and look a little closer to see how he or she can add to the team effort without thought of personal gain.

HONOR: Live up to Army Values.

Honor is a matter of carrying out, acting, and living the values of loyalty, duty, respect, selfless service, integrity, and personal courage in everything you do. It is always doing what you know is right even when no one is looking.

INTEGRITY: Do what's right, legally and morally.

Integrity is a quality you develop by adhering to moral principles. Once lost, it is the hardest to recover. It requires complete honesty in your words and actions. As your integrity strengthens, so does the trust others place in you. Trust is one of the most important attributes in our Profession. The more choices you make based on integrity, the more this highly prized value will characterize your relationships with Family and friends, and finally, define you as a person and a Soldier.

PERSONAL COURAGE: Face and overcome fear, danger, or adversity (physical or moral).

Personal courage has long been associated with our Army. Courage is a matter of enduring physical duress and at times risking personal safety. Facing fear or adversity may require continuing forward on the right path, especially if taking those actions is not popular with others. You can build your personal courage by daily standing up for and acting upon the things that you know are right.

3-5. Suicide Prevention

Everyone has the power and responsibility to protect Soldiers on and off the battlefield. This includes recognizing uncharacteristic and suicidal behaviors.

Effective suicide prevention requires everyone in the unit to be aware of the risk factors for suicide and know how to respond. Commanders, NCOs, supervisors and <u>battle buddies</u> must lead the way.

If a Soldier seems suicidal, the time to take action is NOW. Talk to the Soldier before it is too late.

What to look for: Warning Signs

Distress can lead to the development of unhealthy behaviors. People closest to the Soldier (fellow Soldiers, Family, friends) are in the best position to recognize changes due to distress and to provide support.

Ask your buddy
- Have the courage to ask the question, but stay calm
- Ask the question directly: Are you thinking of killing yourself?

Care for your buddy
- Calmly control the situation; do not use force; be safe
- Actively listen to show understanding and produce relief
- Remove any means that could be used for self-injury

Escort your buddy
- Never leave your buddy alone
- Escort to chain of command, Chaplain, behavioral health professional, or primary care provider
- Call the National Suicide Prevention Lifeline

National Suicide Prevention Lifeline: 1-800-273-8255 (TALK)

USAPHC http://phc.amedd.army.mil

GTA 12-01-003

Look For:
- Comments that suggest thoughts or plans of suicide
- Rehearsal of suicidal acts
- Giving away possessions
- Obsession with death and dying
- Uncharacteristic behaviors
- Significant change in performance
- Appearing overwhelmed by recent stressor(s)
- Depressed mood; hopelessness
- Withdrawal from social activities

3-6. The Soldier's Creed and Warrior Ethos

The Soldier's Creed captures the essence of what it means to be a Soldier.

The Warrior Ethos—within the Soldier's Creed—describes a Soldier's selfless commitment to the nation, the mission, and fellow Soldiers.

All Soldiers are warriors—prepared, trained and fully equipped for war. Soldiers destroy the enemy in close combat, resolve conflict, and then restore the peace. They are also part of a team, bound to each other by integrity and trust.

As Soldiers, you will always be under some level of physical and mental stress, regardless of your rank or specialty. Living by the Soldier's Creed and Warrior Ethos provides the inner strength and motivation you need to continue performing your duty and executing your mission.

The Soldier's Creed

I am an American Soldier.

I am a warrior and a member of a team.

I serve the people of the United States and live the Army Values.

I will always place the mission first.

I will never accept defeat.

I will never quit.

I will never leave a fallen comrade.

I am disciplined, physically and mentally tough, trained and proficient in my Warrior tasks and drills.

I always maintain my arms, my equipment and myself.

I am an expert and I am a professional.

I stand ready to deploy, engage, and destroy the enemies of the United States of America in close combat.

I am a guardian of freedom and the American way of life.

I am an American Soldier.

3-7. The BCT / One Station Unit Training (OSUT) / Advanced Individual Training (AIT) "Golden Rules"

#1 DO NOT bully, haze, assault or harass a fellow Soldier
- ✓ **DO** help and assist your teammate

#2 DO NOT use vulgar language, rude gestures or discriminate against others
- ✓ **DO** treat everyone with dignity and respect

#3 DO NOT kiss, attempt to kiss or touch a fellow Soldier
- ✓ **DO** respect your teammate's personal space

#4 DO NOT steal or take something that does not belong to you
- ✓ **DO** build trust with teammates through your ethical and disciplined actions

#5 DO NOT go anywhere without your battle buddy
- ✓ **DO** report violations of policies and regulations to your platoon and company leadership

Chapter 4 – BCT / OSUT / AIT

4-1. What to expect

All phases of training build character, instill discipline, reinforce the Army Values, improve physical conditioning, and teach basic combat and occupational skills. All of these contribute in the development of your individual skills and knowledge, resulting in a Soldier capable of serving as a member of a team in your first unit of assignment.

BCT / OSUT / AIT are training courses that transform civilians into Soldiers. Over the course of a number of weeks you will develop the character, commitment, and competence skills and knowledge to succeed as a Soldier.

- BCT – 10 weeks
- 11B/C (Infantryman) OSUT – 13 weeks, 3 days
- 12B (Combat Engineer) OSUT – 14 weeks
- 19D (Cavalry Scout) OSUT – 16 weeks
- 19K (Armor Crewman) OSUT – 15 weeks
- 31B (Military Police Officer) OSUT – 19 weeks, 1 day
- AIT – Varies by Military Occupational Specialty

4-2. The training company – Your unit

Upon arrival to your training company, the Drill Sergeants and cadre will in-process you and assign you to a platoon, which is a group of 60 Soldiers and 3 Drill Sergeants. Your

Drill Sergeants are a mix of highly qualified male and female NCOs with 5-10 years of experience in the Army.

The Company Commander (Captain) is in charge of the Company. The Commander establishes policy and has legal discipline authority over you and all assigned company personnel.

The First Sergeant (1SG), who is the master trainer assists the Commander and supervises the Drill Sergeants and other Soldiers and civilians assigned to the company.

There are typically 12 Drill Sergeants assigned to the company. They are responsible for the training and testing you receive. You will also see a Supply Sergeant (could be a civilian) who is responsible for the linen, pillows, cleaning supplies and the work orders needed to maintain the company.

The training NCO or Training Officer/Executive Officer (XO) is responsible for updating and maintaining training records and the coordination of each day's training events.

4-3. Safe and Secure Environment

The Army provides a safe living and learning environment for all Soldiers. When you arrive at your company you will notice security measures established to protect you and your battle buddies.

Alarms are placed on doors that separate male and female Soldiers. This is to ensure no unauthorized entry during lights out or sleeping hours. Do not prop doors open or allow unauthorized persons to enter your barracks bay or sleeping area.

Cameras are installed in common areas (hallways, stairwells, lobbies, etc.) to assist cadre with identifying any misconduct during all hours of the day and night.

The Army installed hotline telephones in the barracks to assist Soldiers in reporting incidents, seeking help from an outside agency, or to check the weather. These hotlines are located in common areas and have multiple pre-programed lines for Soldiers to report incidents or reach important resources.

Upon arrival to your Basic Combat Training location you will receive a briefing on SHARP and introduced to the individuals who are assigned as the Sexual Assault response Coordinator (SARC) and the Victim Advocate (VA).

These are the NCOs and or civilians that will provide you with contact information to be used if violations are observed during your training.

Their names and contact information are posted throughout the barracks and company area.

Write their names and contact information in the area provided in the front of the Blue Book.

4-4. Drill Sergeants

A Drill Sergeant is a symbol of excellence in initial entry training, is an expert in all warrior tasks and battle drills, lives the Army Values, exemplifies the Warrior Ethos, and most importantly is the epitome of the Army as a Profession.

A Drill Sergeant wears the distinctive "campaign hat" or "bush hat" and is responsible for coaching, counseling, mentoring, and transforming Soldiers like you from a civilian volunteer to a combat-ready Soldier.

When addressing a Drill Sergeant your response will be, yes, Drill Sergeant; no, Drill Sergeant, This is a form of respect to the Drill Sergeant and their position.

Like the distinctive headgear they wear, each Drill Sergeant proudly wears their Drill Sergeant badge on their uniform.

The badge has a specific meaning.

It consists of 13 stars representing the original colonies. The torch, burning brightly in the center, symbolizes liberty. The snake is derived from the original "Don't Tread on Me" serpent, a symbol of American independence during the 18th century. Together with the torch and breastplate, it indicates readiness to defend. The breastplate is a symbol of strength. The green background is a vestment worn under the breastplate and called a Jupon, which represents the new Army. The snake grasps, with it's tail and teeth, a scroll inscribed with the Army's motto "This We'll Defend."

The heritage of the Drill Sergeant and NCO reaches back to the Revolutionary War and carries through to today's Army. Drill sergeants provide inspiration, discipline, and technical competence within unit formations.

DRILL SERGEANT CREED

I am a Drill Sergeant

I will assist each individual in their efforts to become a highly motivated, well disciplined, physically and mentally fit Soldier, capable of defeating any enemy on today's modern battlefield.

I will instill pride in all I train, pride in Self, in the Army, and in Country.

I will insist that each Soldier meets and maintains the Army's standards of military bearing and courtesy, consistent with the highest traditions of the U.S. Army.
I will lead by example, never requiring a Soldier to attempt any task I would not do myself.

But first, last, and always, I am an American Soldier, sworn to defend the Constitution of the United Sates against all enemies, both foreign and domestic.

I am a Drill Sergeant.

4-5. The Soldierization process

Initial Entry Soldiers undergo a five-phase training program that prepares you for the transition from civilian volunteer to Professional Soldier. The advancement through each phase is a major "stepping stone" in your life, because each stage repeatedly tests and pushes you to be the best.

In a highly supervised environment, you will experience training that challenges you physically and mentally. Successful Soldiers model the actions, behaviors, and Army Values exhibited by your Drill Sergeants and AIT Platoon Sergeants.

Each of the five phases is essential. They are identified by colors; each phase signifies a specific turning point in becoming a Soldier.

The Red, White, and Blue phases are part of BCT and the first 9 weeks of OSUT. The Black and Gold phases are part of AIT and the latter weeks of OSUT.

4-6. Military time

Being a Soldier is a **24-hour** a day job, it is only fitting that military time is expressed using 24 hours. As a global military force, the U.S. Army constantly coordinates with bases and personnel located in other time zones. To avoid confusion due to time differences, the military uses Greenwich Mean Time (GMT), commonly referred to as military time.

Civilian Time	Military Time	Civilian Time	Military Time
12:00 Midnight	0000	12:00 Noon	1200
12:01 AM	0001	1:00 PM	1300
1:00 AM	0100	2:00 PM	1400
2:00 AM	0200	3:00 PM	1500
3:00 AM	0300	4:00 PM	1600
4:00 AM	0400	5:00 PM	1700
5:00 AM	0500	6:00 PM	1800
6:00 AM	0600	7:00 PM	1900
7:00 AM	0700	8:00 PM	2000
8:00 AM	0800	9:00 PM	2100
9:00 AM	0900	10:00 PM	2200
10:00 AM	1000	11:00 PM	2300
11:00 AM	1100	11:59 PM	2359

4-7. Daily schedule

Typical schedule during BCT/OSUT:

0500 – First Call
0530 – Physical Readiness Training
0630 – Breakfast
0830 – Training
1200 – Lunch
1300 – Training
1700 – Dinner
1800 – Drill Sergeant Time
2030 – Personal Time
2130 – Lights-Out

4-8. Basic Combat Training (BCT)

Red Phase. You begin the Soldierization process by learning discipline, standards, values, and teamwork. In

Red phase, you will learn about the Warrior Ethos, first aid, sexual harassment/assault response and prevention programs, customs and courtesies, and resiliency techniques. You will also participate in physical readiness training, road marches, confidence building exercises, and learn how to march in a military formation. At the end of Red phase you will earn the Army unit patch that is worn on the left shoulder of your ACU uniform.

White Phase. You will learn rifle marksmanship and qualify on your assigned weapon. You will also continue your physical readiness training along with negotiating an obstacle course and train in the field on the basic soldier skills necessary to meet the needs of an expeditionary Army known as" Warrior Tasks and Battle Drills".

These skills help develop your confidence in becoming a strong member of the Army team. At the end of white phase you will earn your rifle qualification badge.

Blue Phase. This phase builds upon what you learned over the past two phases and reinforces the basic combat skills with a focus on teamwork and discipline. You will learn to operate additional weapons used by the Army. You will throw live hand grenades, train in urban operations and survive multiple days in a field environment.

After passing all your BCT tests and challenges, you qualify to wear the Army Black Beret as a Rite of Passage.

4-9. Warrior Tasks and Battle Drills

The Army has identified various basic Warrior Tasks and Battle Drills (WTBDs) that all Soldiers are required to train in order to succeed on the battlefield. These WTBDs are taught in basic combat training and cover critical skills associated with the ability to shoot, move, communicate, and survive.

While in the Reception Battalion, you received a copy of the Soldier's Manual of Common Tasks, Warrior Skills Level 1 (STP-21-1-SMCT). This manual covers all of the WTBDs you are required to know.

Shoot: You will become proficient with your weapon and learn how to maintain, employ, and engage targets as well as how to properly handle and employ hand grenades.

- Maintain, employ, and engage targets with individually assigned weapon system
- Employ hand grenades

Move: You will learn how to move tactically on the ground by practicing individual movement techniques. You will learn how to navigate from one point to another and how to move as a member of a team.

- Perform individual movement techniques
- Navigate from one point to another
- Move as a member of a Team

Communicate: Communication training focuses on using modern technology to convey information effectively. You will learn equipment and procedures to become a more technically savvy Soldier and an effective communicator.

- Perform voice communications
- Use visual signaling techniques

Survive: Experience in handling the pressures of modern warfare is critical for Soldier survival. Practice in survival tasks helps you to react properly to hostile fire, enemy threats, and to maintain situational awareness.

- React to chemical, biological, radiological, and nuclear attack/hazard
- Perform immediate lifesaving measures
- Perform counter Improvised Explosive Device
- Maintain Situational Awareness
- Assess and Respond to Threats (Escalation of Force)
- Construct an Individual Fighting Position

Battle Drills: A battle drill is a collective action performed by a platoon, squad, or team that requires no planning, but is conducted as routine action when events dictate a response.

- React to contact
- Establish security at the halt
- Perform Tactical Combat Casualty care
- React to Ambush (near/far)

4-10. BCT graduation requirements

You must successfully accomplish the following requirements to graduate from Basic Combat Training...

✓ Complete the Army physical fitness test (APFT) by scoring at least 50 points in each event.

In order to graduate from OSUT/AIT you must score at least 60 points in each event. [Goal is to achieve 80 points or higher for your age/gender.]

- ✓ Safely handle, provide proper maintenance, zero, and qualify with your individual weapon using a M68 optic.
- ✓ Demonstrate proficiency in the wear of the chemical protective mask and complete the protective mask confidence exercise (CBRN 2).
- ✓ Pass the end-of-cycle "hands-on" test and demonstrate proficiency in the Warrior Tasks and Battle Drills.
- ✓ Demonstrate proficiency in basic First Aid techniques.
- ✓ Negotiate the obstacle and confidence courses.
- ✓ Complete combatives training.
- ✓ Qualify on the hand grenade qualification course to standard and throw two live hand grenades.
- ✓ Complete the end of cycle 16K tactical foot march.
- ✓ Pass the 3/4-person team Land Navigation Course.
- ✓ Complete the tactical field training and/ or situational training exercises (FTXs/STXs).
- ✓ Complete the Buddy Team Live Fire.

4-11. AIT/OSUT

Transition from BCT to AIT: Soldiers are to report to AIT on the scheduled report date. Soldiers who are authorized to travel to the AIT location with family members must arrive at the AIT location no later than 1800 on the Sunday prior to the scheduled AIT report date. Do not expect passes or privileges above what you were allowed in BCT, ensure you maintain any equipment you were issued, maintain paperwork, and any publications issued during BCT.

In AIT and the final phases of OSUT, you will be trained in your selected MOS (job training) and continue the physical conditioning required for you to excel in your future unit.

During Black and Gold phases, you will receive classroom instruction, hands-on training, and field training to enable you to become a valued team member as you transfer to your first unit of assignment.

Black Phase. The Black Phase or sometimes referred to as "Phase IV" is the first phase of comprehensive MOS training that occurs during weeks 10-13 of OSUT and the initial start of AIT.

This phase will begin to develop your skills in your Army specialty through hands-on training, classroom instruction, and opportunities to apply those skills during various training exercises.

During Personal Financial Management Training, you will receive 8 hours of specialized training in how to handle your finances. Upon completion of the finance training, you will be issued a certificate. Ensure you take this certificate to your first unit of assignment, or you will be required to retake the training.

Gold Phase. The Gold Phase or sometimes referred to as "Phase V" is the final and most progressive stage that covers weeks 14-20+ of OSUT/AIT and the longer periods associated with specific MOSs.

The phase might end with a tactical FTX/STX where you will apply the knowledge and experience you gained from basic combat training and most recent MOS training and apply it in a simulated combat environment.

Graduation requirements.

You must successfully accomplish the following requirements to graduate from One Station Unit Training / Advanced Individual Training...

- ✓ Complete the Army physical fitness test (APFT) by

scoring at least 60 points in each event.
- ✓ Pass MOS-specific critical tasks as identified by the proponent school.
- ✓ Complete the 8 hour personal financial training course.
- ✓ Complete the Army Traffic Safety Training Program
- ✓ Individually pass the High Physical Demand Tests (HPDT) associated with your MOS (AR 611-1)

During your entry into the Army, your training, and/or final phases of AIT/OSUT, if you visually appear to be marginal or exceed body fat content standards, IAW Army Regulation (AR) 40-501 Body Fat Standards, you will be taped in order to determine your body fat percentage. If you exceed the body fat standards you will have six months (180 days) upon entering the Army to meet weight/body fat compliance with AR 600-9.

4-12. What is the difference between Drill Sergeants and AIT Platoon Sergeants?

In AIT, you will be assigned to a different unit and will now have AIT Platoon Sergeants and Squad Leaders instead of Drill Sergeants.

The difference between Drill Sergeants and AIT Platoon Sergeants is the environment in which they train you. Your basic combat training experience will be highly supervised by Drill Sergeants as you are encouraged and evaluated on your ability to reach the highest Army standards. The Drill Sergeant enforces standards and their focus is on "attention to detail". Their job is to ensure you are mentally and physical fit to earn your place as a member of a team and be able to contribute as a soldier in AIT.

During AIT and the latter portion of OSUT, your training environment changes to one that best prepares you for your first unit of assignment. You will learn MOS skills and additional Soldier skills in an atmosphere geared to prepare you for the performance of that occupational specialty in a unit.

The roles of Drill Sergeants and AIT Platoon Sergeants are comparable even though they train Soldiers during different phases of initial entry training. Drill sergeants transform new recruits into Soldiers

AIT Platoon Sergeants, Squad Leaders and MOS Instructors train Soldiers to become proficient at their Army job/MOS and prepare them for their transition to their first assignment.

Your Platoon Sergeant will counsel and mentor you to help develop your skills as a soldier and a member of the team. The AIT Platoon Sergeant is normally a sergeant first class, but can be a staff sergeant and has 3-4 squad leaders that assist him/her in your development. The AIT Platoon Sergeant will assist you in making scheduled appointments, help with assignment instructions, any training or family issues, and provide guidance throughout your AIT training. As you process to your first unit you will continue to be assigned to a platoon and fall under a Platoon Sergeant and squad leaders.

AIT Platoon Sergeants help Soldiers transition from a completely supervised environment to one that involves more individual responsibility. This gives you a better understanding of the duties, discipline, and responsibilities you must maintain as a Soldier.

AIT PLATOON SERGEANT CREED

I AM AN AIT PLATOON SERGEANT

I embody the Army Values and adhere to the highest standards of ethical conduct. I will share my knowledge and experience, and enforce the Army Standards in every Soldier by demonstrating character, competence, and commitment.

I will reinforce Warrior Task and Battle Drills, ensuring all Soldiers are prepared to win the wars of this great nation.

I am physically fit, an effective communicator and a sound administrator. I will never ask my Soldiers to do anything I would not do myself.

It is an honor to guide Soldiers through the transition process. I am a leader and will always conduct myself as a professional.

I AM AN AIT PLATOON SERGEANT

Chapter 5 – Personal Appearance and Uniforms

5-1. Personal appearance

The Army is a profession. A Soldier's appearance measures part of his or her professionalism. Proper wear of the Army uniform is a matter of personal pride for all Soldiers. It is indicative of esprit de corps and morale within a unit.

Soldiers have an individual responsibility to ensure their appearance reflects the highest level of professionalism. Your uniform is only part of your appearance. To look like a Soldier, you need to be physically fit, meet acceptable weight standards, and have a neat hairstyle in accordance with Army regulations.

Note: While attending BCT/OSUT/AIT some of the personal appearance allowances may be restricted while undergoing training. Your Drill Sergeants, AIT Platoon Sergeants and instructors will inform you of these restrictions.

Note: Reference AR 670-1 or DA PAM 670-1 for additional inquiries concerning Army uniforms and awards.
http://armypubs.army.mil/epubs/pdf/r670_1.pdf

Note: When traveling from BCT to AIT wear of the Army Combat Uniform (ACU), or appropriate civilian attire, unless restricted by the commander.

Hairstyles

While at BCT, you will receive a standard haircut. The purpose of the short cut is for hygiene purposes and extensive physical and outdoor activities you will undertake over the next 10 weeks.

Once you graduate from BCT, you may have individualized haircut, as long as it conforms to Army regulation. Most Army Air Force Exchange Store (AAFES) barbers have a poster which shows authorized haircut styles.

Male Grooming Standards

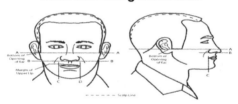

For male personnel, the hair must not fall over the ears or eyebrows, or touch the collar (except for closely cut hair at the back of the neck).

- Hair should be tapered, except that "block cut" in the back is permitted in moderate degree.
- Neither the bulk nor length of hair may interfere with the wearing of military headgear.
- Sideburns must be neatly trimmed, not flared, not come to a point, and must not extend downward beyond the lowest part of the exterior ear opening.

- The face must be clean-shaven.
- If a mustache is worn after graduation from BCT/OSUT/AIT, it must be neatly trimmed.
- No part of the mustache will cover the upper lip line or extend horizontally beyond or below the corner points of the mouth where the upper and lower lips join.

For female personnel, the requirements for hair regulations to maintain uniformity within a military population for female Soldiers while in uniform, or in civilian clothes on duty, unless otherwise specified. Female hairstyles may not be eccentric or faddish and will present a conservative, professional appearance. For the purpose of these regulations, female hairstyles are organized into three basic categories: short length, medium length, and long length hair.

Short length. Short hair is defined as hair length that extends no more than 1 inch from the scalp (excluding bangs). Hair may be no shorter than 1/4 inch from the scalp (unless due to medical condition or injury), but may be evenly tapered to the scalp within 2 inches of the hair line edges. Bangs, if worn, may not fall below the eyebrows, may not interfere with the wear of all headgear, must lie neatly against the head, and not be visible underneath the front of the headgear. The width of the bangs may extend to the hairline at the temple.

Medium length. Medium hair is defined as hair length that does not extend beyond the lower edge of the collar (in all uniforms), and extends more than 1 inch from the scalp. Medium hair may fall naturally in uniform, and is not required to be secured. When worn loose, graduated hair styles are acceptable, but the length, as measured from the end of the total hair length to the base of the collar, may not exceed 1 inch difference in length, from the front to the back. Layered hairstyles are also authorized, so long as each hair's length, as measured from the scalp to the hair's end, is generally the same length giving a tapered appearance. The regulations for the wear of bangs detailed above, apply. No portion of the bulk of the hair, as measured from the scalp, will exceed 2 inches.

Long length. Long hair is defined as hair length that

extends beyond the lower edge of the collar. Long hair will be neatly and inconspicuously fastened or pinned, except that bangs may be worn. The regulations for the wear of bangs detailed above, apply. No portion of the bulk of the hair, as measured from the scalp, will exceed 2 inches (except a bun, which may extend a maximum of 3 inches from the scalp) and be no wider than the width of the head. Long length hair may be worn in a ponytail **during** physical training. A single pony tail centered on the back of the head is authorized only when within the scope of physical training, except when considered a safety hazard. The pony tail is not required to be worn above the collar. When hair securing devices are worn, they will comply with the guidelines. Hairstyles otherwise authorized in this chapter (such as braids and twists) may also be worn in a ponytail during physical training.

Braids, cornrows, and twists. Medium and long hair may be styled with braids, cornrows, or twists (see glossary for definitions). Each braid, cornrow, or twist will be of uniform dimension, have a diameter no greater than 1/2 inch, and present a neat, professional, and well-groomed appearance. Each must have the same approximate size of spacing between the braids, cornrows, or twists. Each hairstyle may be worn against the scalp or loose (free-hanging). When worn loose, such hairstyles must be worn per medium hair length guidelines or secured to the head in the same manner as described for medium or long length hair styles. Ends must be secured inconspicuously. When multiple loose braids or twists are worn, they must encompass the whole head. When braids, twists, or cornrows are not worn loosely and instead worn close to the scalp, they may stop at one consistent location of the head and must follow the natural direction of the hair when worn back, which is either in general straight lines following the shape of the head or flowing with the natural direction of the hair when worn back with one primary part in the hair. Hairstyles may not be styled with designs, sharply curved lines, or zigzag lines. Only one distinctive style (braided, rolled, or twisted) may be worn at one time. Braids, cornrows, or twists that distinctly protrude (up or out) from the head are not authorized.

Dreadlocks or locks. Female Soldiers may wear dreadlocks/locks in accordance with the guidance for braids, cornrows, and twists.

Jewelry

A wrist watch, identification bracelet, and up to two rings (a wedding set is considered to be one ring) may be worn with your uniform as long as they are conservative and tasteful. Soldiers may also wear one activity tracker, pedometer, or heart rate monitor. You may wear a religious medal on a chain around your neck provided neither medal nor chain can be seen.

Earrings may be screw-on, clip-on, or post-type earrings, in gold, silver, white pearl, or diamond. The earrings will not exceed 6 mm or 1/4 inch in diameter, and they must be unadorned and spherical. When worn, the earrings will fit snugly against the ear. Females may wear earrings only as a matched pair, with only one earring per ear lobe.

Note: Females are not authorized to wear earrings with any class C (utility) uniform (ACU, hospital duty, food service, physical fitness, field, or organizational).

Body Piercing

Except for earrings worn by female Soldiers when wearing the ASU, no displaying objects, articles, jewelry, or ornamentation attached or affixed to or through the skin may be worn while in uniform. Neither can such adornments be worn while wearing civilian clothes (on or off duty) when on any military installation, or other places under military control. When females are not in uniform and off duty, earring wear is not restricted as long as the earrings do not create or support ear gauging (enlarged holes in the lobe of the ear, greater than 1.6mm).

Cosmetics

Standards regarding cosmetics are necessary to maintain uniformity and to avoid an extreme or unprofessional appearance. Males are prohibited from wearing cosmetics, except when medically prescribed. Females are authorized to wear cosmetics with all uniforms, provided they are applied modestly and conservatively, and that they complement both the Soldier's complexion and the uniform. Leaders at all levels must exercise good judgment when interpreting and enforcing this policy.

Eccentric, exaggerated, or faddish cosmetic styles and colors, to include makeup designed to cover tattoos, are inappropriate with the uniform and are prohibited. Permanent makeup, such as eyebrow or eyeliner, is authorized as long as the makeup conforms to the standards outlined above. Eyelash extensions are not authorized unless medically prescribed.

Females will not wear shades of lipstick that distinctly contrast with the natural color of their lips, that detract from the uniform, or that are faddish, eccentric, or exaggerated.

Females will comply with the cosmetics policy while in any military uniform or while in civilian clothes on duty.

Fingernails

All personnel will keep fingernails clean and neatly trimmed.

Males will keep nails trimmed so as not to extend beyond the fingertip.

Females will not exceed a nail length of 1/4 inch, as measured from the tip of the finger. Females will also trim nails shorter if the commander determines that the longer length detracts from the military image, presents a safety concern, or interferes with the performance of duties. Females may wear clear acrylic nails, provided they have a natural appearance and conform to Army standards.

Tattoos

Note: Violation of tattoos policy by Soldiers may result in adverse administrative action and/or charges under the provisions of the Uniform Code of Military Justice (UCMJ).

Tattoos and brands are permanent markings that are difficult to reverse (in terms of financial cost, discomfort, and effectiveness of removal techniques). Before obtaining either a tattoo or a brand, Soldiers should consider talking to unit leaders to ensure that they understand the Army tattoo and brand policy. The words tattoo and brand are interchangeable in regards to this policy.

The following types of tattoos or brands are prejudicial to good order and discipline and are, therefore, prohibited anywhere on a Soldier's body:

- Extremist. Extremist tattoos or brands are those affiliated with, depicting, or symbolizing extremist philosophies, organizations, or activities. Extremist philosophies, organizations, and activities are those which advocate racial, gender, or ethnic hatred or intolerance; advocate, create, or engage in illegal discrimination based on race, color, gender, ethnicity, religion, or national origin; or advocate violence or other unlawful means of depriving individual rights under the U.S. Constitution, and Federal or State law (see AR 600–20).

- Indecent. Indecent tattoos or brands are those that are grossly offensive to modesty, decency, propriety, or professionalism.
- Sexist. Sexist tattoos or brands are those that advocate a philosophy that degrades or demeans a person based on gender.
- Racist. Racist tattoos or brands are those that advocate a philosophy that degrades or demeans a person based on race, ethnicity, or national origin.

Tattoos or brands, regardless of subject matter, are prohibited on certain areas of the body as follows: Soldiers are prohibited from having tattoos or brands on the head, face (except for permanent makeup, neck (anything above the t-shirt neck line to include on/inside the eyelids, mouth, and ears), wrists, hands, except Soldiers may have one ring tattoo on each hand, below the joint of the bottom segment (portion closest to the palm) of the finger. Accessing applicants must adhere to this same policy.

- Soldiers may not cover tattoos or brands with bandages or make up in order to comply with the tattoo policy.

5-2. Army Combat Uniform (ACU)

Boots

New boots should fit properly when you receive them.

- They should have a chance to air out between uses, so you should wear one pair one day and another pair the next.
- Scrape dirt or mud from boots and wash with just a little water and soap.
- Wipe insides dry with a clean cloth and remove all soapsuds from the outside.
- Stuff paper in the toes and let boots dry in a warm, dry place.
- Do not put boots in the hot sun or next to a strong source of heat.
- Let boots dry.
- Heels of boots should be replaced after wear of 7/16 of an inch or more.

Insignia placement

Each Soldier is responsible for having the correct insignia properly placed on their uniform, as follows:

Shoulder sleeve insignia.

Soldiers in both BCT and AIT who are in one of the following categories may wear organizational shoulder sleeve insignia. Wear this insignia centered on the left sleeve.

Subdued shoulder sleeve insignia will be worn on all field and work uniforms.

- Army National Guard (ARNG) and United States Army Reserve (USAR) trainees are authorized to wear the insignia of their parent ARNG or USAR organization from the start of training.

- Unit-of-choice trainees are authorized to wear, from the start of training, the insignia of the specific unit for which they enlisted.

"U.S. ARMY" insignia: ACU

- Worn immediately above and parallel to the top edge of the left chest pocket.

- This insignia consists of black, 3/4-inch high block letters on a 1-inch wide by 4-1/2 inch long (or to the edges of the pocket flap) strip. The background can be either olive green or the universal camouflage pattern.

Name tape: ACU

- Worn immediately above and parallel to the top edge of the right chest pocket of all field and work uniform coats and shirts.

- It consists of black letters on a 1-inch wide by 4-1/2 inch long (or to the edges of the pocket flap) strip of cloth.

- Names of 10 letters or less will be printed in 3/4-inch high Franklin Gothic Condensed.

- Names of 11 letters or more will be printed in 1/2-inch high Franklin Gothic Extra Condensed.
- The name and U.S. Army tapes will be the same length.

Grade insignia: Army Combat Uniform / Operational Camouflage Pattern (OCP)

Soldiers wear subdued (cloth) last name and U.S. Army identification insignia attached to Velcro. Grade insignia is attached to Velcro area provided in center of the jacket flap. Soldier may sew on the U.S Army tape, name tape, rank and all authorized badges, as an option.

Rank insignia placement

Belts and Buckles

The rigger, sand or tan 499 rigger belt will be worn with the ACU (OCP).

The rigger belt is worn with the attached black, open-faced buckle. It is worn so that the tipped end passes through the buckle to the wearer's left; the end will not extend more than 2 inches beyond the edge of the buckle. The belt's end may be neatly trimmed to ensure a proper fit. Information of Army Uniforms is located in Army Regulation 670-1
http://www.apd.army.mil/pdffiles/p670_1.pdf

Operational Camouflage Pattern Army Combat Uniform (ACU)

- Soldiers are authorized to wear the Operational Camouflage Pattern ACU starting 1 July 2015. Sales will begin July 2015. Centralized issue for incoming Soldiers will begin January 2016 (2QFY16). Mandatory possession date is 1 October 2019.

- Soldiers are authorized to wear the sand or the Tan 499 T-shirt, sand or Tan 499 belt, and tan or Coyote Brown boots during the transition period which ends 30 SEP 2019.

- Tan 499 T-shirt color:
  Available starting July 2015.

- Tan 499 belt color:
  Available starting July 2015.

- Coyote Brown boot color:
  Available starting August 2015.

NOTE: Soldiers may only wear OEF-CP headgear with the OEF-CP Flame Resistant Army Combat Uniform and Operational Camouflage Pattern headgear with the Operational Camouflage Pattern Army Combat Uniform.

The Improved Outer Tactical Vest (GEN II) Video Donning Doffing:
https://www.youtube.com/watch?v=1CtmLG45k_A&feature=youtu.be

5-3. Army Service Uniform (ASU)

ALL MALES
Center regimental crest 1/8 inch above the top of the pocket flap. Wear the Crest 1/4 inch above unit awards and foreign badges, if worn.

ALL SOLDIERS
Center unit awards 1/8 inch above the top of the pocket flap (males), and center unit awards with the bottom edge 1/2 inch above the top of the nameplate (females).

ALL MALES
Center the nameplate on the flap of the right pocket, between the top of the button and the top of the pocket.

All ENLISTED
Place the bottom of the branch insignia disk (approximately 1 inch for males and 5/8" for females) above the notch, centered on the left collar with the centerline of the insignia parallel to the inside edge of the lapel. Place the U.S. insignia disk on the right collar in the same position

ALL SOLDIERS
Center marksmanship badges on the pocket flap 1/8 inch (males) below the seam and 1/4 inch below the ribbons (females). If more than one badge is worn, space them 1 inch apart. When special skill badges are worn place them to the right of marksmanship badges.

ALL SOLDIERS
Coat sleeve ornamentation enlisted (both males and females). Enlisted personnel have a 1/8" soutache braid of gold colored nylon or rayon on each sleeve.

Enlisted ASU (Male)

ALL ENLISTED
Distinctive Unit Insignia (enlisted personnel only) Enlisted personnel wear the DUI on the ASU coat, centered on the shoulder loops an equal distance from the outside shoulder seam to the outside edge of the button, with the base of the insignia toward the outside shoulder seam.

ALL ENLISTED
Center rank insignia between the shoulder seam and the elbow on both sleeves.

ALL SOLDIERS
Center unit awards 1/8 inch above the top of the pocket flap (males); and center unit awards with the bottom edge 1/2 inch above the top of the nameplate (females).

ALL SOLDIERS
OSBs - if authorized for wear.

The overseas service bar is worn centered on the outside bottom half of the right sleeve of the Army Service Uniform coat. The lower edge of the overseas service bar is placed 1/4 inch above the right sleeve braid of the coat for officer personnel, and 4 inches above and parallel to the bottom of the sleeve for enlisted personnel. Each additional bar is spaced 1/16 inch above, and parallel to the first bar.

ALL ENLISTED
Center service stripes on the outside of the left sleeve 4 inches from the bottom. Place the service stripe at a 45-degree angle with the lower end toward the inside seam of the sleeve.

ALL SOLDIERS
The front crease of the slacks or trousers will reach the top of the instep and be cut on a diagonal line to reach a point approximately midway between the top of the heel and the top of the standard shoe in the back. The slacks or trousers may have a slight break in the front.

ENLISTED BRAID
Trouser leg (males) enlisted corporal and above have one 1-1/2 inch gold-colored nylon or rayon braid.

Trouser leg (females)
enlisted corporal and above have one 1-inch gold-colored nylon or rayon braid.

Enlisted ASU (Female)

Grade Insignia: ASU

- The Army white shirt may be worn with or without the ASU coat, which is known as the Class B uniform.
- E-4s (Specialists) and below must always wear their grade insignia on the collars of the white shirt.
- Corporals and above must wear shoulder board grade insignia on the white shirt.

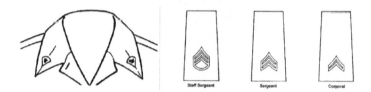

Grade Insignia, Enlisted Shirt

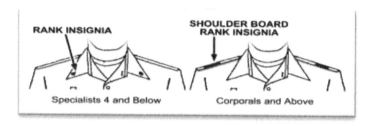

Male - U.S. and branch insignia

During initial entry training, males will wear the "U.S." insignia disk on both collars.

The bottom of the insignia disk will be approximately 1-inch above the notch where the collar meets the lapel, centered between the seam and the outside edge of the collar. The "U.S." or branch insignia will be canted parallel to the inside edge of the lapel on the ASU coat.

After completing AIT or OSUT, male Soldiers will wear military occupational specialty branch insignia on their left collar.

On the male ASU jacket, the nametag will be worn on the right pocket flap, centered between the top of the pocket and the top of the button, centered on the flap and parallel to the ground.

Regimental crest will be worn 1/8-inch above the top of the right pocket and centered.

Ribbons will be worn 1/8-inch above the top of the left pocket, centered on the pocket, and parallel to the floor.

Qualification badges will be worn 1/8-inch down from the top of the pocket and centered on the flap with at least 1-inch between badges if two are worn, and evenly spaced if three are worn.

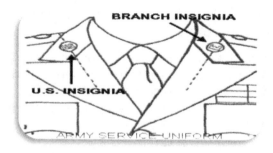

U.S and Branch Insignia, Enlisted Male

Female - U.S. and branch insignia

During initial-entry training, females will wear the "U.S." insignia on both collars.

The bottom of the insignia disk will be worn approximately 5/8-inch above the notch where the collar meets the lapel, centered between the seam and the outside edge of the collar. The "U.S." or branch insignia will be positioned parallel to the inside edge of the lapel on the ASU coat.

After completing AIT or OSUT, female Soldiers will wear military occupational specialty branch insignia on their left collar.

On the female ASU coat, the bottom edge of the nameplate will be 1 to 2 inches above the top of the top button, centered on the right side of the uniform and parallel to the ground.

The regimental crest will be worn ½-inch above the name plate or ¼ inch above any unit awards or foreign badges that are worn.

The bottom edge of the ribbons will be parallel to the bottom edge of the name plate, and centered on the jacket.

The Qualification badges will be ¼ -inch below and centered on the ribbons, with 1-inch between badges.

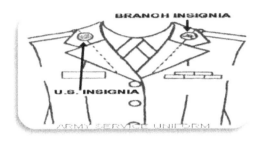

U.S and Branch Insignia, Enlisted Female

Belts and Buckles

The belt issued to Soldier's to wear with the ASU is black webbed with a nickel under-plate for males and black cotton web for females.

Patrol Cap

The patrol cap is the standard headgear worn with the combat uniform in the garrison environment. The patrol cap has a visor, circular top crown, side crown with an outside crown band, and a hook-and-loop pad on the back of the patrol cap

Soldiers will wear the patrol cap straight on the head so that the cap band creates a straight line around the head, parallel to the ground. The patrol cap will fit snugly and comfortably around the largest part of the head without bulging or distortion from the intended shape of the headgear and without excessive gaps. No rolling of, blocking, or alterations to the cap are authorized. Rank insignia will be wore center front of the cap between the top seam and the bottom seam

Beret

The beret is worn so that the headband (edge binding) is straight across the forehead, 1 inch above the eyebrows.

The flash is positioned over the left eye, and the excess material is draped over to the right ear, so it is extended to at least the top of the ear, and no lower than the middle of the ear.

Wear of Beret (Male and Female)

Personnel will cut off the ends of the adjusting ribbon and secure the ribbon knot inside the edge binding at the back of the beret.

When worn properly, the beret is formed to the shape of the head; therefore, Soldiers may not wear hairstyles that cause distortion of the beret.

Note: IET Soldiers will not wear unit insignia on the beret until they arrive at their first unit of assignment.

5-4. Awards and Decorations

Personal Decorations and Awards

Personal decorations and awards are bestowed upon an individual for his or her act of heroism, specific act of gallantry, or for meritorious service during military or non-military feats.

Collective (Unit) Citations

Collective citations are made to an operating unit for outstanding performance inside or outside of the U.S. It is worn by only those persons who were members of that unit during the action or period specified by the award.

Medals Commemorative, campaign, and service medals are issued to Soldiers who take part in particular campaigns or periods of service for which a medal is authorized.

Ribbons representing the medals issued are normally worn on the ASUs. Some units, such as the 3rd Infantry (Old Guard) wear the full-size medals on their uniforms.

Ribbons

The *Army Service Ribbon* is awarded to Soldiers who successfully complete OSUT or AIT. More information can be found in AR 600-8-22.

Marksmanship Badges

Marksmanship badges are awarded to individuals who qualify, because they have demonstrated some special proficiency or skill. Marksmanship badges are worn to indicate the individual's prowess with specific weapons, pistols, and/or rifles and during specified competitions, matches, or practice exercises. You will earn one of the marksmanship badges during BCT.

Expert   Sharpshooter   Marksman   Clasp (typical)

Chapter 6 – Critical Information Required for BCT / OSUT / AIT

6-1. Rank Insignia

Military customs and courtesies dictate that you render the appropriate greeting and salute to officers when you encounter them in the performance of your duties.

This chart can assist you in understanding the Army rank structure. The individual's title reflects the rank of the person. You should never address a person by their pay grade.

Title	Pay Grade	Rank	Remarks
Private (PVT)	E-1	No Chevron	
Private (PV2)	E-2		
Private First Class (PFC)	E-3		

Specialist (SPC)	E-4		

NCOs are "the backbone" of the Army. They are responsible for executing a military organization's mission and serve as the principal instructor for training military personnel so they are prepared to execute those missions.

Senior NCOs are considered the primary link between enlisted personnel and the commissioned officers. If they are the senior NCO in a staff section they may be referred to as an NCO-in-charge (NCOIC). Their advice and guidance is particularly important for junior officers, who begin their careers in a position of authority but generally lack practical experience.

Corporal (CPL)	E-4		A SPC recognized with NCO authorities
Sergeant (SGT)	E-5		Team leader

Staff Sergeant (SSG)	E-6		Squad leader or section chief
Sergeant First Class (SFC)	E-7		Senior NCO in a platoon
Master Sergeant (MSG)	E-8		NCOIC at battalion and brigade
First Sergeant (1SG)	E-8		Senior NCO in a company; advisor to the commander
Sergeant Major (SGM)	E-9		Principal advisor on a battalion and higher HQs staff
Command Sergeant Major (CSM)	E-9		Senior enlisted advisor at battalion and higher HQs

Sergeant Major of the Army (SMA)	E-9		Senior NCO in the Army; advisor to the Chief of Staff of the Army

<u>Warrant Officers</u> are highly specialized technicians and trainers in their career fields. By gaining progressive levels of expertise and leadership, these leaders provide valuable guidance to commanders and subordinate Soldiers in their units.

Warrant Officer 1 (WO1)	W-1		Company and battalion staffs
Chief Warrant Officer 2 (CW2)	W-2		Company and battalion staffs
Chief Warrant Officer 3 (CW3)	W-3		Company and higher staffs
Chief Warrant Officer 4 (CW4)	W-4		Battalion and higher staffs

| Chief Warrant Officer 5 (CW5) | W-5 | | Brigade and higher staffs |

Commissioned Officers are responsible for planning and leading demanding missions while ensuring the welfare, morale and professional development of the Soldiers entrusted to them.

At the Captain, Lieutenant Colonel and Colonel level they may serve as commanders for companies, battalions and brigades. In that capacity, they have disciplinary authorities over you under the Uniformed Code of Military Justice.

2nd Lieutenant (2LT)	O-1		Platoon Leader
1st Lieutenant (1LT)	O-2		Company Executive Officer
Captain (CPT)	O-3		Company Commander; Battalion Staff Officer

Major (MAJ)	O-4		Battalion Executive Officer; Brigade Staff Officer
Lieutenant Colonel (LTC)	O-5		Battalion Commander; Division Staff Officer
Colonel (COL)	O-6		Brigade Commander; Division Staff Officer

General Officers are commissioned officers who serve as commanders at division-size units and larger, as commanders of installations, and as principal advisors to senior national and state civilian leaders and higher-ranking general officers.

Brigadier General (BG)	O-7		
Major General (MG)	O-8		

| Lieutenant General (LTG) | O-9 | ★★★ | |
| General (GEN) | O-10 | ★★★★ | |

6-2. Customs and Courtesies

Saluting

The origin of the hand salute is uncertain. Some historians believe it began in late Roman times when assassinations were common. A citizen who wanted to see a public official had to approach with his right hand raised to show that he did not hold a weapon. Knights in armor raised visors with the right hand when meeting a comrade. This practice gradually became a way of showing respect and in early American history sometimes involved removing the hat. By 1820, the motion was modified to touching the hat, and since then has become the hand salute used today.

While in the Army, you salute to show respect toward an officer, flag, or our country. The proper way to salute with or without a weapon is described in Training Circular (TC) 3-21.5, paragraph 4-4. When to salute is covered by Army Regulation (AR) 600-25.

Follow these rules:

When you meet someone outside, salute as soon as you recognize that he or she is an officer, or if you are walking toward the officer, wait until you are about <u>six steps away</u>.

Salute all officers (recognized by grade) in official vehicles identified by special plates or flags.

Salute only on command when in a formation.

If in a group and an officer approaches, the first Soldier to recognize the officer calls the group to attention and all personnel salute.

If you approach an officer while you are double-timing alone, assume quick time, render the hand salute and give the proper greeting. When the salute is returned, execute order arms and resume double-time.

The salute is always initiated by the subordinate and terminated only after acknowledgment by the individual saluted.

Accompany the salute with an appropriate greeting, such as, **"Good morning/afternoon, sir /ma'am."**

Salutes are not required to be rendered by or to personnel who are driving or riding in privately owned vehicles.

It is not customary for enlisted personnel to exchange salutes, except in some ceremonial situations.

Never render a salute with a noticeable object in your mouth or right hand.

If you are on detail and an officer approaches, salute if you are in charge of the detail. Otherwise, continue to work. When spoken to, come to the position of attention while addressing an officer.

Hand salute

The Hand Salute is a one-count movement. The command is **Present, ARMS.** The Hand Salute may be executed while marching. When marching, only the Soldier in charge of the formation salutes.

When wearing headgear with a visor (with or without glasses), on the command of execution **ARMS,** raise the right hand sharply, fingers and thumb extended and joined, palm facing down, and place the tip of the right forefinger on the rim of the visor slightly to the right of the right eye. The outer edge of the hand is barely canted downward so that neither the back of the hand nor the palm is clearly visible from the front. The hand and wrist are straight, the elbow inclined slightly forward, and the upper arm horizontal.

When wearing headgear without a visor (or uncovered) and not wearing glasses, execute the Hand Salute in the same manner as previously described, except touch the tip of the right forefinger to the forehead near and slightly to the right of the right eyebrow.

When wearing headgear without a visor (or uncovered) and wearing glasses, execute the Hand Salute in the same manner as previously described, except touch the tip of the right forefinger to that point on the glasses where the temple piece of the frame meets the right edge of the right brow.

Order Arms

Order Arms from the Hand Salute is a one-count movement. The command is **Order**, **ARMS.** On the command of execution **ARMS,** return the hand sharply to the side, resuming the Position of Attention.

When reporting or rendering courtesy to an individual, turn the head and eyes toward the person addressed and simultaneously salute. In this situation, the actions are executed without command. The Salute is initiated by the subordinate at the appropriate time (six paces) and terminated upon acknowledgment.

Rendering customs and courtesies to NCOs and Warrant Officers

When addressing an NCO you will need to be at the position of Parade Rest. The NCO may direct you to At ease, Stand at Ease; or Rest.

When walking with someone of higher rank, walk on the left side of the individual.

Always greet individuals with the greeting of the day.

Be respectful at all times.

Warrant Officers will be treated in the same respect as Officers.

Rendering Honor to the Flag

The flag of the U.S. is the symbol of our nation. The union, white stars on a field of blue, is the honor point of the flag. The union of the flag and the flag itself, when in company with other flags, are always given the honor position, which is on the right.

The flag of the U.S. is displayed outdoors at all Army installations.

The flag is displayed daily from reveille to retreat. If illuminated, it may be displayed at night during special events or on special occasions deemed appropriate by the commander.

When the flag is being raised in the morning or lowered in the evening, stand at attention on the first note of Reveille or "To the Color." "Color" refers to the flag of the U.S. and can include the unit flag. Give the required salute. You normally face the flag when saluting, unless duty requires you to face in some other direction. At the conclusion of the ceremony, resume your regular duties.

The flag, when flown at half-staff, is hoisted to the peak/top of the flagpole and then lowered to the half-staff position. At the end of the day, the flag is hoisted to the peak before lowered. "Half-staff" means lowering the flag to one-half the distance between the top and bottom of the staff.

Whenever Reveille or To the Color is played, and you are not in formation and not in a vehicle, come to attention at the first note, face the flag, and give the required salute. If no flag is near, face the music and salute. If you are in formation, salute only on the order "Present arms." If you are in civilian clothing, stand at attention and place your right hand over your heart.

Courtesies

The following rules will help you conduct yourself appropriately in the presence of officers and those senior in grade:

When talking to an Officer or Warrant Officer, stand at attention unless given the order "At ease." When you are dismissed, or when the officer departs, come to attention and salute.

When an officer enters a room, the first Soldier to recognize the officer calls personnel in the room to attention but does not salute. When a Soldier reports indoors render a salute to the officer.

When accompanying a senior, walk on his left.

When an officer enters a dining facility, unless he directs otherwise or a more senior officer is already present, the diners will be given the order "At ease" by the first person who sees the officer. You will remain seated at ease and will continue eating unless the officer directs otherwise. If you are directly addressed, you should rise to attention when seated in a chair. If you are seated on a bench, stop eating and sit at attention until the conversation ends.

Note: The officer or NCO may give the directive "Carry on." This means the Soldier or Soldiers should continue with whatever they were doing previously. This same directive is used in many other situations outside of formation, such as in the barracks and break areas.

When outdoors and approached by an NCO, you should stand (when seated) and greet the NCO by saying, "Good morning, sergeant," "Good afternoon, sergeant," or "Good evening, sergeant (last name, if known)."

While going through BCT, you will address all Drill Sergeants as "Drill Sergeant".

When you report to an officer and you are outdoors, approach the officer, stop about two steps from him, and assume the position of attention. Give the proper salute and say, for example, "Sir/Ma'am, Private Smith reports." If you are indoors, use the same procedures as above, except remove your headgear before reporting.

6-3. Bugle Calls

Bugle calls are the musical signals that announce scheduled and certain non-scheduled events on an Army installation. Scheduled calls are prescribed by the installation commander. According to Army customs, bugle calls traditionally signal troops for everything from meal times and recall formations, to rendering honors to the nation. Bugle calls normally sound in accordance with the major calls of the day-Reveille, Retreat, and Taps.

Reveille

The call signals the troops to awaken for morning roll call. Most often heard at physical training, it is used to accompany the raising of the National Colors. If outdoors at the first sound of Reveille, you should come to the position of attention and salute, facing the flag or the sound of the music. If not in uniform, come to attention and place your right hand over your heart.

Retreat

The call signals the end of the duty day and lowering of the National Colors. If alone, you should come to attention in the direction of the music or flag. Then, salute when you hear the first note of music after the cannon sounds. If not in uniform, come to attention and place your right hand over your heart.

Taps

The call signals that unauthorized lights are to be extinguished. It is the last call of the day. The call is also sounded at the completion of a military funeral ceremony. You should come to attention and salute until the music completes. If not in uniform, come to attention and place your right hand over your heart.

6-4. Drill and Ceremonies

Many drill procedures used by the U.S. Army today were developed during the Revolutionary War. The purpose of the drill then was to instill discipline in American Soldiers. As these Soldiers mastered the art of the drill, they began to work as a team and develop a sense of pride in themselves and in their unit.

In today's Army, the same objectives–teamwork, confidence, pride, alertness, attention to detail, esprit de corps, and discipline are accomplished by drill.

A drill consists of a series of movements by which a unit or individuals are moved in an orderly, uniform manner from one formation or place to another. Units vary in size, but in BCT, you will ordinarily be part of a squad, platoon, company or battalion.

You will need to know the following drill terms:

Element is an individual, squad, section, platoon, company, or larger unit formed as part of the next higher unit.

Formation is an arrangement of the unit's elements in a prescribed manner such as a line formation in which the elements are side-by-side, or a column formation in which the elements are one behind the other. In a platoon column, the members of each squad are one behind the other with the squads abreast.

Front is a space from one side to the other side of a formation, and includes the right and left elements.

Depth is a space from the front to the rear of a formation, including the front and rear elements.

Distance is the space between elements that are one behind the other. The distance between individuals is an arm's length, plus 6 inches, or approximately 36 inches measured from the chest of one Soldier to the back of the Soldier immediately to his front.

Interval is the space between side-by-side elements.

Rank is a line that is only one element in depth.

File is a column that has a front of one element.

Guide is the person responsible for maintaining the prescribed direction and rate of march.

Post is the correct place for an officer or NCO to stand in a prescribed formation.

Head is a column's leading element. **Base** is the element

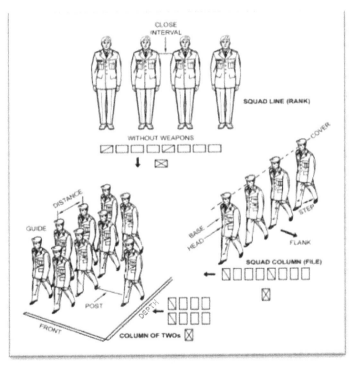

around which a movement is planned or regulated.

Cadence is a uniform rhythm or number of steps or counts per minute.

Quick Time is a cadence of 120 counts (steps per minute).

Double Time is a cadence of 180 counts (steps per minute).

Drill commands are oral orders given by your commander or leader, usually in two parts. The preparatory command states the movement to be carried out and gets you ready to execute the order. The command of execution tells when the movement is to be carried out. In the command "Forward, march," the *preparatory* command is "Forward," the command of *execution* is "March."

In some commands, the preparatory command and the command of execution are combined. For example, "Fall in," "at ease," and "Rest." These commands are given without inflection and at a uniformly high pitch and loudness comparable to that of a normal command of execution.

If you are in a group of three or more, marching is required when moving from one location to another.

Most marching movements are a five-step process. This can be simplified into the acronym PICAA:
P-preparatory command
I-intermediate step
C-command of execution
A-action step
A-additional step.

Put simply, the Preparatory command, the Command of execution and the Action step—executing the movement—are all given or executed when the same foot strikes the marching surface. The Intermediate step and Additional step are executed with the other foot.

Chapter 7 – Physical Readiness

As a Soldier, you are required to maintain a high level of personal readiness and resilience. Optimal personal readiness in building and maintaining the Soldier Athlete requires you to get sufficient sleep, maintain physical fitness and strength, and fuel your body with the right diet. These three key attributes (sleep, activity, and nutrition) are often described as the Performance Triad.

The Performance Triad along with regular hygiene and resilience skills ensure you are prepared to perform at the elite level regardless of your MOS/Duty.

You can get more information on the Performance Triad at http://armymedicine.mil/Pages/performance-triad.aspx. A smartphone application for both iphone and android platforms is available.

7-1. Army Physical Fitness Uniform (APFU)

The components of the APFU are:
1. Jacket, running, black and gold.
2. Pants, running, black.

3. Trunks, running, black, moisture-wicking.
4. T-shirt, black, short sleeve, moisture-wicking.
5. T-shirt, black, long sleeve, moisture-wicking.
6. Cap, knit, black

The only insignia authorized for wear on the APFU is the Physical Fitness Badge. When the physical fitness badge is worn, it is sewn on the upper left front side of the APFU T-shirt. On the APFU running jacket, the insignia is sewn centered 1/2 inch above the word "Army."

Soldiers are authorized to wear commercially purchased black spandex shorts under the APFU trunks. The length of the shorts must end above the knee or higher. The commercial shorts must be plain, with no logos, patterns, or obtrusive markings. Soldiers are not required to buy spandex shorts. This is an optional purchase.

Only pregnant Soldiers are authorized to wear the APFU shirt outside of the trunks.

Commanders may authorize the wear of commercial running shoes, calf-length or ankle-length plain white/black socks with no logos, gloves, reflective belts or vests, long underwear, and other items appropriate to the weather conditions and type of activity. If Soldiers wear long underwear or other similar items, they must conceal them from view when wearing the running jacket and pants of the APFU.

7-2. Army physical fitness test (APFT)

References:
- FM 7-22, Army Physical Readiness Training
- DA Form 705, Army Physical Fitness Test Scorecard

The intent of the APFT is to provide an assessment of your physical readiness.

Physical Fitness testing is designed to ensure that every Soldier is maintaining a high level of physical performance, regardless of MOS or duty assignment.

7-3. APFT Standards.

Push-Ups

PU Points	Age 17-21 M	Age 17-21 F	Age 22-26 M	Age 22-26 F	Age 27-31 M	Age 27-31 F
100	71	42	75	46	77	50
80	57	31	58	32	58	34
60	42	19	40	17	39	17
50	35	13	31	11	30	10

Sit-Ups

SU Points	Age 17-21 M	Age 17-21 F	Age 22-26 M	Age 22-26 F	Age 27-31 M	Age 27-31 F
100	76	76	80	80	82	82
80	66	66	65	65	64	64
60	53	53	50	50	45	45
50	47	47	43	43	36	36

2-Mile Run

2-Mile Points	Age 17-21		Age 22-26		Age 27-31	
	M	F	M	F	M	F
100	13:00	15:36	13:00	15:36	13:18	15:48
80	14:24	17:12	14:48	17:36	15:06	18:12
60	15:54	18:54	16:36	19:36	17:00	20:30
50	16:36	19:42	17:30	20:36	17:54	21:42

APFT Scorecard – Your Progress...

Points	#1		#2		#3	
	Event	Score	Event	Score	Event	Score
PU						
SU						
Run						
Total						

The APFT provides a measure of upper and lower body muscular endurance. It is a performance test that indicates a Soldier's ability to perform physically and handle his or her own body weight. APFT standards are adjusted for age and physiological differences between male and female.

The APFT consists of three events:
1. Push-ups
2. Sit-ups
3. 2-mile run

The events are performed in that order and on the same day. Soldiers are allowed a minimum of 10 minutes and a maximum of 20 minutes rest between events. All three events must be completed within two hours.

Soldiers in BCT must attain 50 points in each event and an overall score of 150 points to meet APFT minimum standards. You should push yourself to achieve your maximum performance in each event.

Soldiers in AIT and OSUT must attain a score of at least 60 points on each event and an overall score of at least 180 points to graduate.

The maximum score a Soldier can attain on the APFT is 300 points. This should be your goal.

Chapter 8 – Health and Safety

8-1. Nutrition

Fuel the body for optimal performance

As a Soldier, you are expected to achieve and maintain a high level of fitness – physical and mental. Fitness is not only achieved by your training, but also by how you fuel your body. Fueling with the wrong foods will lead to mental and physical fatigue and could play a large part in injuries and illnesses. The right kinds of food can be found in Army dining facilities and in the civilian world—optimal fueling requires a little knowledge, a little restraint, and a dedication to the Army Ethos that you have chosen.

Remember: You can't "out-exercise" a poor diet.

Fueling with the right amount of carbohydrates, protein, and healthy fats promotes energy, endurance, stamina, and muscle growth. Benefits of proper fueling include:

- **Maintaining a healthy weight**
- **Decreasing post-exercise muscle soreness**
- **Stronger and healthier muscles**

To create a winning eating pattern, keep these concepts in mind:

1. Eat at least 3-5 different kinds of nutrient-dense foods at each meal. The more types of food you eat, the more vitamins, minerals, and other nutrients you

consume.

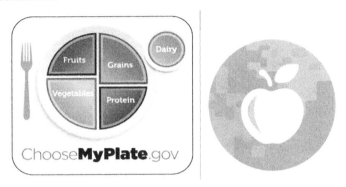

Five Food groups- Mealtime Visual.

General guidelines are to have:

½ of your plate full of a variety of fruits and vegetables

¼ of your plate composed of complex carbohydrates

¼ of your plate in the form of protein.

Portion sizes will vary based on your energy needs and performance goals.

Think in terms of the following:

Energy: Fuel your body with complex carbohydrates and healthy fats.

2. Enjoy all foods in moderation. Aim for an eating pattern

that provides 85-90% nutrient-dense foods, and 10-15% foods with fewer nutritional merits.

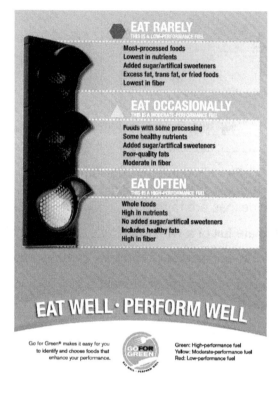

The Go For Green® labeling program in the dining facilities can assist you in choosing nutrient-dense foods.

3. Make an effort to choose minimally processed, wholesome foods.

- **Whole grains and starches** are the foundation of a high performance eating pattern. Grains are an excellent sources of carbohydrates, fiber, and B vitamins. They are the primary fuel for your muscles and brain, protect against muscular fatigue, and can reduce problems with constipation if high in fiber.

- **Sources**: Whole-grain cereals (i.e. Total®, Cheerios™, Kashi®, Shredded Wheat, Granola), oatmeal, whole-grain bread, brown rice, and quinoa

- **Vegetables** are excellent sources of vitamin C, beta-carotene, potassium, magnesium, and many other vitamins, minerals, and other health-protective substances. Fresh vegetables are the best, but frozen vegetables are also a good second choice.
Sources: raw or cooked broccoli, spinach, peppers, tomatoes, carrots

- **Fruits** add to the strong carbohydrate foundation for your performance eating pattern. Fruits are rich in fiber, potassium, and many other vitamins, especially vitamin C. The nutrients found in fruits can aid in recovery after exercise and improve healing. **Sources**: whole fruit (i.e. bananas, apples, oranges, grapes), 100% fruit juice, dried fruit

- **Protein rich foods** from animal and plant sources should be eaten as a complement to the carbohydrate found in fruits, vegetables and grains. These foods provide the amino acids you need to build and repair muscles.
<u>Sources</u>: chicken and turkey, fish, lean beef (i.e. top round, eye of round, round tip), peanut butter, legumes (i.e. kidney beans, black beans, etc.), and soy protein (i.e. tofu)

- **Dairy and calcium-rich foods** are a quick and easy sources of protein, vitamin D, and calcium. Calcium and vitamin D help to maintain strong teeth and bones.
<u>Sources</u>: low-fat (1%) or nonfat milk (skim), low-fat or nonfat yogurt, green leafy vegetables

4. Eat the right kinds of fat.

- **Limit intake of "hard" saturated fats**
<u>Sources</u>: fat found on animal protein, butter

- **Use more "soft" unsaturated fats**
<u>Sources</u>: olive oil, canola oil, fish, avocado, peanut butter, nuts and seeds

- **Avoid *trans* fats (partially hydrogenated oils)**
<u>Sources</u>: found in commercially prepared foods such as crackers, cakes, cookies, chips, and pastries

Stay Hydrated

Fluid needs vary greatly from person to person, and depend on intensity of work, level of heat stress, and sweat rates. The first step to being well hydrated is to drink fluids and eat foods high in water content throughout the day. Cool water is the beverage of choice for maintaining hydration. Recommended fluid intake ranges from 2 to 5 quarts per day.

You may have a need for extra salt (a source of sodium) depending on the severity of sweat loss and the degree in which you are adapted (acclimatized) to the heat*. The consumption of food and beverages and adding salt to foods are the preferred methods to replacing sodium losses.

Sports drinks may be an option for sodium replacement if you are not consuming enough food during training and/or you are not acclimated to the heat*. Avoid putting sports drinks in your wearable hydration system, as this will increase the risk of harmful bacteria or mold growth.

*NOTE: heat acclimatization may take up to 21 days or more for untrained Soldiers.

ARE YOU HYDRATED?
TAKE THE URINE COLOR TEST

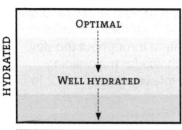
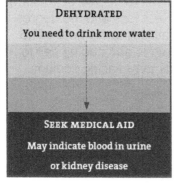

This color chart is not for clinical use.

Some vitamins and supplements may cause a darkening of the urine unrelated to dehydration.

The simplest way to determine if you are adequately replacing the fluid lost through sweat is to check the color and quantity of your urine. If your urine is dark and scanty, you need to drink more fluids or eat more foods with a high water content

Fluids = water, sports drinks, 100% fruit juice, milk, milk alternatives (soy, almond)

Foods = high-water-content fruits and vegetables, soup, yogurt

Be smart about energy drinks

Energy drinks are not the same as sports drinks and should never be used for hydration — cool, plain water should always be a first choice for hydration. Energy drinks generally contain large quantities of caffeine and may contain other ingredients, most of which do absolutely nothing to enhance performance or health. Also, the large quantities of caffeine can actually aggravate dehydration, and may also lead to increased anxiety, upset stomach, shakiness, headaches, and sleep issues.

These potential side effects can actually reduce your ability to perform, NOT enhance it. Instead of reaching for energy drinks, it's best to feed your body energy throughout the day:
- Snack on carbohydrates and energy-rich foods such as dried fruits, nuts, trail mix, a commercial sports bar or low-fat chocolate milk.
- Drink cool, plain water frequently, even if you aren't thirsty.

Dietary supplements
Many Soldiers use dietary supplements to improve performance, increase muscle mass, enhance energy, accelerate recovery, increase alertness, boost their immune system, and improve joint function. However, dietary supplements are not tested or approved by the Food and Drug Administration prior to being placed on the market, are often unnecessary, and can be dangerous and expensive.

OPERATION SUPPLEMENT SAFETY

Operation Supplement Safety (OPSS) is a joint initiative between the Human Performance Resources Center (HPRC) and the Department of Defense (DoD) to educate Service Members and retirees, their family members, leaders, healthcare providers, and DoD civilians about dietary supplements and how to choose supplements wisely. The OPSS website (https://www.opss.org/) provides easy access to updated materials and databases for you to stay informed and make healthy dietary supplement choices.

8-2. Sleep

The disciplined practices in *sleep*, *activity*, and *nutrition* comprise the Army's "performance triad." By following the habits outlined below you will do the most for yourself to maximize performance, and avoid illness and injury.

Make Sleep A Priority - Sleep is a biological need for brain functioning and is critical for sustaining the mental abilities required for success in basic combat training and advanced individual training. Soldiers require a minimum of 7-8 hours of sleep every 24-hours.

In basic combat training, you will have the opportunity for at least 7 hours of continuous sleep per night (unless you are scheduled for duty such as access control guard/fireguard or charge of quarter's runner).

During field training, the length of the training day and time for sleep will vary based on training requirements; however, your commander will ensure that the schedule allows sufficient time for sleep during field training.

The MOST IMPORTANT THING YOU MUST REMEMBER: When you have the opportunity to sleep, do it. Insufficient sleep presents a risk to mission success. Sleep deprived Soldiers are likely to make mission critical and sometimes fatal errors.

The demanding nature of military operations often creates situations in which obtaining enough sleep on a regular basis is difficult or impossible. Such chronic, insufficient sleep (anything less than 7—8 hours per 24) produces a sleep debt – a chronic state of increased sleep need that is characterized by impaired performance and readiness.

The only way to eliminate the debt is to obtain sleep (just closing your eyes and resting is not the same as sleeping/napping). As a Soldier you must make sleep a priority!

When you have the opportunity to rest or sleep, do it.

8-3. Activity

During BCT you will obviously maintain a high level of activity. However once you graduate from AIT or OSUT, you will have much more control over your level of activity. You will need recreational-type activities to maintain your optimum performance; Army physical readiness training and the other high-physical demands of your duties will not provide all the physical activity you need.

Physical activity is more than just "exercise" or "working out"- it's living an active lifestyle. Whether it's walking the dog, doing yard work, or playing with your kids, regular movement throughout the day inspires positive health outcomes over time.

Physical activity improves health in the following ways:

- Lowers risk of some chronic diseases and conditions such as type 2 diabetes, high blood pressure, stroke, and cancer (e.g. breast, colon).
- Aids in weight loss and prevents weight gain.
- Helps manage stress and may reduce depression.
- Strengthens bones, muscles, and joints.
- Boosts confidence and self-esteem.

Amount and types of physical activity. To receive positive health outcomes you need at least:

- 150 minutes of moderate-intensity aerobic activity per week. 150 minutes is also: 2 hours & 30 minutes per week OR 30 minutes a day for 5 days OR 10 minutes of activity 3 times a day for 5 days.
- 2 days of muscle strengthening activities (e.g. weight/resistance band training, calisthenics, yoga).
- 10,000 steps during your everyday routine. (*Note:* 10,000 steps is close to 5 miles. An inactive person may only average 1,000 to 3,000 steps a day, or about one mile. Persons who walk no farther than this in a normal day should add walking to their routines.

Save time by bumping up the intensity. Do 75 minutes of vigorous-intensity activities per week (e.g., jogging, swimming laps, or hiking uphill).

- Pick activities you enjoy. Moderate-intensity activities include: brisk walking, doubles tennis, golf, and leisure biking.
- Invite Family, friends, and fellow Soldiers to join you. Take a fitness class, join a recreation league, sign up for a 5K run/walk, or start a walking group in your neighborhood.

8-4. Hygiene

In addition to Army training, personal hygiene plays a crucial role in your overall physical readiness as a strong, productive Soldier. There are numerous health concerns that can arise if you do not conduct proper personal hygiene at home and in field environments.

Hazard of communicable diseases

Communicable diseases are caused by specific infectious organisms like viruses or bacteria transmitted from one person to another. The person who is infected may feel sick and look sick, or might carry the illness without feeling or looking sick. These diseases can rapidly degrade the medical readiness of military units and their ability to carry out their mission. They can also cause significant suffering and overwhelm the military health care system.

You received vaccinations to protect you against the increased risk of these infections when you entered the Army, and you will receive additional vaccinations prior to traveling to foreign areas. There are many communicable illnesses that do not have vaccines such as, the common cold and hepatitis C and D.

Resistance to illness

Vaccines do part of the job; the rest is up to you. You are immune to most illnesses most of the time because of your own immune system. It continues with things you do to protect yourself, like keeping yourself and your environment clean; wearing a clean uniform appropriate for the season; and avoiding contact with persons who are ill. Also, you should always cough into your arm and clean your hands frequently to avoid spreading/receiving germs.

Immediate hazards to your health

Do not take chances with your health. If in doubt, get medical help. Injuries that pose a threat to your health or life are:

- Any eye injury
- Any human or animal bite that breaks the skin
- Allergic reaction to an insect bite, chemicals, or medications
- Bleeding that cannot be stopped
- Burns, including severe sunburn
- Feeling very hot and/or confused after being out in the heat
- Exposure to cold temperatures and you think you may have a cold injury

Other symptoms of illnesses that can threaten your health or life include:

- Tightness, pressure, or pain in your chest that spreads to your neck, jaw, arm, or back
- Shortness of breath, or wheezing while resting

- Difficulty breathing, or the feeling of choking
- Coughing up blood
- Difficulty speaking, swallowing, or opening your mouth
- Stiff neck with fever
- Sudden loss of vision
- Very bad pain anywhere on your body
- Weakness and dizziness
- Blood in your urine or brown urine
- Vomiting up blood or what looks like coffee grounds
- Blood in your stool or black, tar-like stools
- You feel like you might hurt yourself or others
- Hip or knee injuries
- Painful teeth or swelling in your mouth or jaw

If you experience any injuries or symptoms of illness, report them to your Drill Sergeant immediately to get health care.

Bathe / shower daily

Regular bathing with soap and water is important for both cleanliness and personal appearance.

Bathing prevents hygiene-related diseases such as scabies, ringworm, athlete's foot, skin infections, and pink eye.

You should especially wash your hands, face and ears, armpits, groin, and feet. In addition to washing your skin regularly you should wash your hair at least twice a week, shave daily and, avoid sharing combs or razors with others.

Wash hands regularly

Normally your immune system protects you against invasion by bacteria, viruses, and parasites; however, if your hands become contaminated with these organisms and you put them up to your nose or mouth, disease germs can invade your body and cause an infection.

Many aspects of basic training can make you more vulnerable to respiratory illnesses, including close contact with other Soldiers.

The physical and psychological stresses of military training can make you more vulnerable to illness. In addition, your immune system may not be ready to withstand the new organisms you are exposed to when first brought together as a group.

Almost 90 percent of Soldiers get symptoms of respiratory illness at some point during basic combat training. In most cases, these illnesses are mild and trainees are able to continue training, but sometimes they progress to worse infections like pneumonia or meningitis.

Washing your hands with soap and water is the most effective way to prevent the spread of bacteria and viruses which are major cause of food borne diseases and other illnesses. Although the use of hand sanitizers is effective for killing most of these harmful organisms on the hands, they are ineffective on hands that are heavily soiled with dirt, grease, and other debris. Therefore the use of hand sanitizers should not be used in place of hand washing, rather as a supplement to or a temporary alternative when hand washing is not available.

Wash or sanitize your hands every time:
- After using the latrine
- Before eating or handling food
- After sneezing or blowing your nose

It is important to practice good hygiene habits when you are in basic training, because it will become more difficult to wash your hands and bathe regularly when you are in the field or deployed.

Dental health and readiness

Brush and Floss Your Teeth.

Keeping your mouth healthy maintains your dental readiness, and ensures that you won't suffer from pain, infection, or inability to eat high-performance foods. Poor oral health takes more Soldiers out of the fight than the enemy does.

Wisdom teeth and gum disease cause problems, but most dental emergencies are caused by tooth decay or its complications.

Tooth decay is usually caused by bacteria (germs) that feed on starchy or sugary snacks and beverages, and by acids that wear away the surfaces of teeth. Soda, juice, sweet tea, sports drinks and energy drinks all contain sugar and acids that can damage teeth.

Saliva is critical for protecting your teeth from decay by neutralizing acids, hardening teeth, and fighting germs.

Stressful training or operations can decrease saliva flow, leaving you vulnerable to decay.

Prevent dental problems in two ways: watch what you put in your mouth, and clean your mouth every day.

Watch what you put in your mouth.

Follow the guidelines in the Nutrition section above, and you will contribute toward a healthy mouth.

Your teeth and gums need the same water intake, calcium, vitamins and minerals, and protein that the rest of your body does, as well as protection from sugars, acid content, and simple starches.

In addition to a healthy diet:

- If you drink sugary drinks, make sure they are cold and minimize contact with your teeth. You can use a straw that reaches to the back of your tongue, or just chug the drink down all at once.
- Rinse your mouth with plain water after drinking sugary drinks

- If you drink juice, choose juice that has calcium added, to minimize acid damage.
- Use xylitol-sweetened gum or mints for 5-10 minutes after meals and snacks to fight cavities.
- Avoid tobacco. Tobacco can cause gum disease and oral cancer.
- Use lip balm with sunscreen during sun exposure to prevent lip cancer.

Clean your mouth every day:

- Brush 2 - 3 times a day, every day, with fluoride toothpaste to remove food particles and harmful bacteria from your teeth. Fluoride helps repair early stage tooth decay.
- Brush before going to sleep to provide greater protection for your teeth.
- Use a soft or ultrasoft toothbrush that is small enough to fit around your back teeth.
- Brush your teeth for about 2-3 minutes using a gentle, circular motion. Pay extra attention to the gum-line, back teeth, and areas around fillings, crowns or bridges.
- Brush your tongue and the roof of your mouth to remove germs that cause tooth decay and bad breath.

- If you have an appliance such as an orthodontic retainer or partial denture, remove it before brushing your teeth. Brush all surfaces of the appliance also.
- Do not rinse your mouth after brushing. Just spit several times to remove excess toothpaste.
- Don't eat or drink anything for at least 30 minutes after you brush so the fluoride will stay on your teeth longer and protect them better
- If you can't brush:
- Swish with water after eating or drinking.
- Wipe your teeth with a clean cloth wrapped around your finger.
- Rub toothpaste on the surfaces of your teeth with your finger.
- Floss once a day. Flossing removes bacteria and food in between teeth, where a toothbrush can't reach
- Use 18 inches of floss. Wrap the end of the floss around your middle finger and use your index finger to guide the floss.
- Insert the floss between your teeth. Pull gently side to side to get it through the tight spots, but be careful not to saw your gums! Use a different area of the floss for each space.

- Gently move the floss up and down against the tooth in back, then the tooth in front.
- Wrap the floss around the teeth as you're moving it up and down.
- Your gums may bleed at first when you start flossing every day. If bleeding continues to happen after a week or two of flossing, see your dentist.

Remember - YOU control whether you get cavities or not!

Whenever a dentist tells you there is a problem at your annual exam, get it treated as soon as possible.

Note: Females should be extra vigilant about brushing with fluoride toothpaste 2 or 3 times a day, to prevent cavities and bleeding gums.

This is because females tend to make less saliva than males, which can leave them more vulnerable to decay.

Fluctuations in female hormones can also negatively affect oral health. Hormones and oral contraceptives can increase bacteria levels in the mouth and cause changes in the blood vessels in the gums, leading to gingivitis.

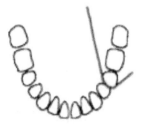

Females who have gingivitis can experience an increase in symptoms during monthly hormonal fluctuations, resulting in tenderness, swelling, and bleeding when brushing.

Females who use oral contraceptives are also twice as likely to develop a dry socket after dental extraction.

Smoking increases this risk.

Hormone fluctuations and stressful environments have been associated with development of painful mouth ulcers or canker sores.

Nutritional deficiencies (vitamins B1, B2, B6, B12, folate, C and iron, magnesium or zinc) may also increase your risk of developing mouth ulcers, so eating fruits and vegetables can help.

Over-the-counter remedies are effective for the discomfort caused by small ulcers. Larger or more painful ulcers may interfere with a normal diet.

A dentist can prescribe medicine to reduce pain and accelerate healing of larger ulcers.

Care for your feet and nails

Athlete's foot is caused by a fungus that lives in damp, warm, and dark areas like shower rooms, rubber boots, and old running shoes.

Athlete's foot usually looks like little blisters between the toes. These can pop, causing itching and little sharp pains. Also, the skin might crack or look scaly.

You can get athlete's foot from walking barefooted on unclean facilities and not washing your feet.

The symptoms include itching, flaking, and cracking between toes or on bottom of feet.

To prevent Athlete's foot, do the following:

- Wear shower shoes while taking showers and when walking on the floor.
- Use a towel to dry thoroughly between your toes.
- Wear clean dry socks; never wear another Soldier's socks.
- Clean the showers and latrine floors daily.
- Sprinkle foot powder in your socks to help absorb the moisture.
- Remove the inserts from your boots at night to prevent fungus from growing.

If you get athlete's foot, you need an anti-fungal solution or cream to treat it.

Wear one pair of boots one day and change to your other pair the next day.

In addition to preventing Athlete's foot, you must also make sure you prevent ingrown toenails. Ingrown toenails are caused by a combination of tight shoes and trimming the toenails down to the edge of the nail.

Symptoms include tenderness, swelling, sharp pain, redness, and discharge.

You can prevent ingrown toenails by trimming nails straight across every two weeks.

Seek medical attention for treatment, for surgery may be necessary to remove the nail from the skin. Cut toenails short and square

Trim Your Toenails

Prevent blisters

Blisters are caused by friction from tight fitting shoes, breaking in new boots, and road marches.

Symptoms are redness and tenderness of the skin.

All blisters cannot be prevented, but they can be minimized.

Wearing proper fitting boots and tight fitting, clean, dry socks free of excessive wear can prevent most blisters.

Second skin (mole skin) on "hot spots," knee-high nylons, and good personal hygiene will help reduce chances of getting a blister as well.

Also, wear work gloves if working with equipment that you will be doing repetitive movements, such as raking or shoveling.

Take the following measures to treat a blister:
- Wash with a mild soap and water and keep your skin clean and dry. Apply a topical anti-biotic ointment to prevent infection.
- Cover with bandage or second skin to prevent from opening.
- DO NOT purposely open a blister.
- If blister opens, treat as you would any open cut.
- Always leave the top skin of a drained blister.

- Pulling off the top layer of skin can damage the new skin underneath and cause infection.

Protect your hearing

Survival on the battlefield could depend on your ability to hear. Hearing loss caused by noise is painless, progressive, permanent, but also preventable.

To protect your hearing, insert your earplugs correctly whenever instructed to wear them.

Do not lose your earplugs. If you do lose your earplugs, notify your Drill Sergeant immediately.

Wear your earplugs to protect your hearing, for you will be glad you did.

Protect against the Effects of Heat and Cold

Protect Against the Effects of Heat, Cold, and Insects.

While you are in BCT and AIT you may be exposed to extremes of heat and cold and biting insects. To protect you from the effects of heat, cold, and insects your cadre will ensure that you have the following things:

- Safeguards against over-stress from heat, or over-exposure to cold, especially in your first couple weeks.
- Water and other beverages, and nutritious meals. You will probably be drinking more water and beverages than you are used to drinking.

- Protective clothing and sunscreen, and insect repellent. Your uniform is factory-treated with a conventional insect repellent for clothing.
- Instructions on what items of your uniform to wear, and how much water you should drink, on a given day.
- Reminders about symptoms and signs of hot and cold weather illnesses, to watch for in both yourself and your buddy.
- Questions about whether you have been ill, or are taking medication, that may increase your risk of heat and cold weather illness.

Note: In case of a severe hot weather illness, your cadre may remove the outer clothing and apply ice water-soaked sheets to the affected Soldier.

Here are a few things to remember all the time:

- Eat all your meals and drink all the water and beverages provided to you. Food and fluids are needed to "fuel" your body's regulating systems for both heat and cold.
- Make sure your uniform is clean, worn as instructed, and all buttons and fasteners are serviceable. Apply sunscreen and insect repellent to your face, neck, and hands as instructed.
- Let your cadre know if you aren't feeling well, taking medications, and/or have unusual insect bite marks

that look infected. Also let your cadre know if you think your buddy is not feeling well.
- Watch the amount and color of your urine as an indicator of whether you are drinking enough water and fluids. This is just as important in cold weather as it is in hot weather.
- When you are in AIT, if you purchase energy drinks, sports drinks, or supplements, ensure that you continue eating all meals and drink all the water and beverages provided to you.

8-5. Ready and Resilient

Soldiers must cope with adversity, perform well in stressful situations, and learn to thrive in stressful environments.

The ready and resilient Fitness program is designed to build resilience and enhance the performance of the Army Family Soldiers, their Families, and Army Civilians – through hands-on training and online self-development tools.

Resilient individuals enhance Army performance and readiness. Resilience is the ability to grow and thrive in the face of challenges and bounce back from adversity.

The goal of ready and resilient Family Fitness is to increase your resilience and enhance your performance by developing and strengthening five dimensions of strength.

1. **Social** strength refers to developing and maintaining trusted, valued relationships and friendships that are personally fulfilling and foster good communication including a comfortable exchange of ideas, views, and experiences.

2. **Emotional** strength means approaching life's challenges in a positive, optimistic way by demonstrating self-control, stamina, and good character with your choices and actions.

3. **Family** strength is about being a part of a Family unit that is safe, supportive and loving, and provides the resources needed for all members to live in a healthy and secure environment.

4. **Spiritual** strength refers to one's purpose, values, beliefs, identity, and life vision. These elements, which define the essence of a person, enable one to build inner strength, make meaning of experiences, behave ethically, persevere through challenges, and be resilient when faced with adversity. An individual's spirituality draws upon personal, philosophical, psychological, and/or religious teachings, and forms the basis of their character.

5. **Physical** strength is about performing and excelling in physical activities that require aerobic fitness, endurance, strength, healthy body composition, and flexibility derived through exercise, nutrition, and training. The physical dimension also encompasses the Office of the Surgeon

General (OTSG) Performance Triad initiative of sleep, activity, and nutrition to improve personal and unit performance, resilience, and readiness.

8-6. Chaplains

The chaplain is responsible for providing spiritual support to every Soldier in the unit. Although chaplains are part of a particular denomination, their mission is to ensure the spiritual needs of every Soldier are met. Each battalion in the Army has its own Chaplain (normally a CPT). The chaplains and their assistants form the Unit's Ministry Team.

Chaplains hold weekly services (while in garrison and in the field), are available for individual counseling, and are one of the few members of the military who retain the privilege of confidentiality. The chaplain also plays a key role in helping promote programs, such as suicide prevention.

In the BCT/OSUT/AIT environment, they are of particular value in helping Soldiers succeed under difficult and stressful conditions. They assist the commander in teaching, displaying, instilling the Army Values, and in maintaining high morale within the unit.

8-7. Risk management

Every Soldier, regardless of rank, is faced with making decisions. You will be challenged to make smart decisions about risk, decisions that will affect not only yourself, but also your team, Family, and friends.

The Army uses a system called Risk Management to help make those decisions. ATP 5-19, *Risk Management* is the Army's doctrinal manual for risk management.

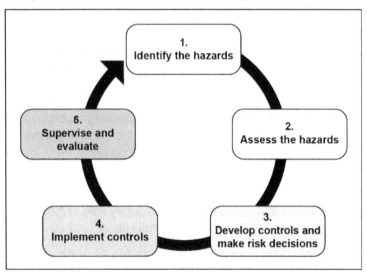

The system doesn't just apply in combat but to everything you do on or off duty. The whole goal is to preserve the Army's ability to fight and win by keeping you safe. The Army's Risk Management is a logical approach to risk-associated decision making that will help you make smart risk decisions and reduce the possibility of becoming a loss.

As you progress throughout your career, you will learn more about the Risk Management process. For now, you need to focus on a few items to ensure your safety while you are in Initial Entry Training:

- Hot Weather Injury Awareness
- Cold Weather Injury Awareness
- Weapon Muzzle Awareness
- Environmental Hazards (insects, animals, poisonous plants, etc.)
- Follow all directions/orders at all times

Chapter 9 – Discipline

The Army is subject to military law and the laws of our government, and we strive to live as law-abiding Soldiers in whatever we do and wherever we go.

Military discipline is founded upon self-discipline, respect for authority, and the embracing of the professional Army ethic with its supporting core values.

Military discipline is developed through individual and group training to create a mental attitude that will result in proper conduct and prompt obedience to lawful military authority.

The Rules

There are three basic rules you should follow:

- Follow Army regulations and the UCMJ.
- Take responsibility for your actions.

- Set the example, do what is right even when no one is watching and always keep your hands to yourself.

While military discipline is the result of effective training, it affects every aspect of military life. It is a characteristic found in individuals and units that demonstrate:

- Unit cohesion, bonding, and a spirit of teamwork.
- Smartness of appearance and action.
- Cleanliness and maintenance of dress, equipment, and quarters.
- Respect to seniors and mutual respect between senior and subordinate personnel.
- Prompt and willing execution of both the letter, and the spirit of the legal orders of their lawful commanders.
- Fairness, justice, and equity for all Soldiers, regardless of age, race, ethnicity, religion, color, gender, or national origin.

9-1. Uniform Code of Military Justice (UCMJ)

The UCMJ is the statute that prescribes criminal law for Soldiers. It applies to active duty Soldiers 24 hours a day and 7 days a week. Anywhere you are in the world, the UCMJ applies.

All persons in the military service are required to strictly obey and promptly execute the legal orders of their lawful seniors.

The UCMJ authorizes non-judicial punishment (administrative actions) by commanders and judicial punishment by court-martial (military courts).

The UCMJ covers traditional offenses that can occur inside or outside of the military environment. Examples include assault, burglary, rape, and murder.

It also provides for the punishment of strictly military offenses. Military offenses are those not common in civilian law. Examples include failure to repair, absence without leave, disrespect to NCOs and commissioned officers, and disobedience of orders.

The principle that an accused is innocent until proven guilty applies to both non-judicial punishment and courts-martial. You have the right to be informed of any charges against you, as well as the names of accusers and known witnesses.

UCMJ: Non-Judicial Punishment

Under the provisions of the UCMJ, Article 15, commanding officers may impose non-judicial punishment upon Soldiers who commit minor offenses within their units.

The purpose of non-judicial punishment is to train, correct, and reform. It also promotes positive behavior changes in Soldiers without the stigma of a courts-martial conviction.

While Article 15s are often considered "minor," common punishments include: <u>revocation of pay</u>, <u>revocation of time (through extra duty)</u> and <u>revocation of rank</u>.

Some of the common UCMJ offenses in IET are:

Refusing to train; disobey a lawful order; disrespect to an officer/noncommissioned officer; sexual harassment/assault, and missing formation.

UCMJ: Court-Martial

There are three types of court-martial: *summary, special,* and *general.*

Trials by court-martial are the military equivalent of civilian trials by judges and juries. The differences among the three are based on their composition, level of authority, and severity of punishments authorized.

A *summary court-martial* is composed of a commissioned officer on active duty with the grade of captain or above. The purpose of the summary court-martial is to make thorough and impartial inquiries into minor offenses and to make sure that justice is done, with the interests of both the government and the accused being safeguarded.

A *special court-martial* consists of a military judge and not less than three panel members when required. It is held for relatively serious offenses.

A *general court-martial* consists of a military judge and not less than five panel members when required. It is held for serious offenses.

A general court-martial may impose any authorized punishment including the death penalty in certain cases.

9-2. Equal opportunity policy

The Equal Opportunity (EO) program ensures an Army-wide, concentrated effort to maximize human potential and to ensure fair treatment for all persons based solely on merit, fitness, and capability in support of readiness.

The EO philosophy is based on fairness, justice, and equity.

The Army's EO program emphasizes fair and equal treatment for military personnel, and civilian employees without regard to race, color, religion, gender, or national origin. This policy applies on and off post, extends to Soldiers, civilian employees, and Family members, and includes working, living, and recreational environments.

Complaint process

The EO complaints processing system addresses grievances that allege unlawful discrimination or unfair treatment on the basis of race, national origin, color, gender, religious affiliation, or sexual harassment.

Attempts should always be made to solve the problem at the lowest possible level within an organization.

If a complaint is submitted, it will be investigated. Those personnel found in violation of the EO Policy are subject to punishment under the UCMJ.

Within reason, Soldiers and other individuals are encouraged to attempt resolution of any complaints by confronting an alleged offender, or by informing other appropriate officials about the offensive behavior or unfair treatment.

Also, individuals are responsible to advise their chain of command on the specifics of any discrimination or sexual harassment so appropriate action can be taken.

Personnel must submit only legitimate complaints, and should exercise caution against frivolous or reckless allegations.

Types of EO complaints

The Army has two types of EO complaints within its EO complaint process: informal, and formal.

An *informal complaint* is any complaint that a Soldier, Family member or DA civilian does not wish to file in writing. Informal complaints may be resolved by the complainant directly with the assistance of another unit member, the commander, or another person in the complainant's chain of command.

Typically, those issues that may be taken care of informally can be resolved through discussion, problem identification, and clarification of the issues. An informal complaint is not subject to time suspense, nor is it reportable.

A *formal complaint* is one that a Soldier, Family member, or DA civilian files in writing and swears to the accuracy of the information. DA Form 7279-R, Equal Opportunity Complaint Form can be obtained at the unit or higher headquarters level.

Formal complaints require specific actions, are subject to timelines, and require documentation of actions taken.

Alternative measures

Although handling EO complaints through the chain of command is strongly encouraged, this is not the only channel. Should a Soldier feel uncomfortable in filing a complaint with the chain of command, or should the complaint be against a member of the chain of command, there are a number of alternative agencies through which a complaint can be made.

The following agencies are frequently used:

- Equal Opportunity Adviser (EOA)
- Chaplain
- Provost Marshal
- Staff Judge Advocate
- Housing Referral Office

- Inspector General
- EO Hotline

Right to Appeal

If a complainant perceives an investigation failed to reveal all relevant facts, or if actions taken on their behalf are perceived as insufficient, he or she has the right to appeal to the next higher commander.

The complainant may not appeal the action taken against the perpetrator, if any is taken.

9-3. Policy on relationships between Soldiers

The Army has historically relied upon customs and traditions to define the bounds of acceptable personal relationships among its members. Soldier relationships have always been judged with reference to customs and traditions of the service.

It is difficult to predict which relationships (strong friendships, parent-child, sibling, career, and business) can create or appear to create an adverse impact on discipline, authority, morale or mission. Therefore, the Army prohibits all unprofessional relationships that compromise the chain of command, cause partiality or unfairness, involve the improper use of grade for personal gain, or are perceived to be exploitive or coercive in nature.

Relationships that may create or appear to create an adverse impact on discipline, authority, morale, or mission accomplishment are also prohibited.

Professional Relationships: Professional relationships are interactions consistent with the Army Values.

Professional relationships are those that contribute to the effective operation of the Army.

Unprofessional Relationship: Unprofessional relationships occur when they detract from the authority of superiors or result in or create the appearance of: favoritism, misuse of office or position, or the abandonment of organizational goals for personal interests.

Unprofessional relationships negatively affect our ability to carry out our mission. History shows unprofessional relationships erode morale, respect for authority, unit cohesion, and mission accomplishment.

Due to the damage to that might occur, maintaining an unprofessional relationship is specifically prohibited and could result in disciplinary action.

Fraternization

The Army's fraternization policy prohibits personal relationships between officer and enlisted personnel regardless of their service. This policy applies to different-gender relationships and same-gender relationships.

Violations of the fraternization and improper relationships policy may be punished under Article 92 and/or 134, UCMJ, as a violation of a lawful general regulation.

Categories of personal relationships may include:
- Dating
- Shared living accommodations
- Engaging in intimate or sexual relations
- Business enterprises
- Commercial solicitations
- Gambling or borrowing
- Writing personal letters
- Text messages
- Emails (Unrelated to the training mission)
- Personal telephone conversations (Unrelated to the training mission)
- Friending through Social media sites

Improper relationships

There are two major categories of illegal associations: relationships between permanent party members and BCT/OSUT/AIT Soldiers (Cadre-Trainee) and relationships between BCT/OSUT/AIT Soldiers (Trainee-Trainee).

Any relationship between permanent party personnel and Trainee Soldiers not required by the training mission is prohibited.

There are no consensual relationships between Cadre-Trainee or between Trainee-Trainee during BCT/OSUT/AIT.

Trainers will sign a form with explicit and strict command guidance that acknowledges their understanding and responsibilities regarding the policies prohibiting inappropriate behaviors and relations outlined in DOD instructions.

This form will be retained in the trainer's record while they are assigned to the training duty and will be revalidated annually.

This includes, but is not limited to, the following:
- Drinking, dancing, or gambling.
- Writing and/or receiving personal letters or emails.
- Riding in permanent party privately owned vehicles.

- Having sexual conversations, contact (kissing, hugging, caressing, fondling, handholding, etc.), or intercourse.
- Sending and/or receiving text messages or phone calls.
- Personal telephone conversations (Unrelated to the training mission)
- Friending through Social media sites

IET Soldiers are prohibited from having any relationship with permanent party personnel without regard to the installation assignment of the permanent party member or the trainee.

For example, personnel assigned or attached to the U.S. Army Recruiting Command may not have any relationship with potential prospects, applicants, and members of the Delayed Entry Program or Delayed Training Program, not required by the recruiting mission.

After receiving the training on the policies stated in the DOD instructions all Soldiers will sign a form with explicit and strict command guidance acknowledging their understanding and responsibilities as outlined in the instructions.

This form will be retained in the Soldier's file until they detach from the training command or school to which they are assigned or attached.

Unlawful associations between Trainee Soldiers involve any actual or attempted consensual contact or socializing between or among Soldiers who are BCT/OSUT/AIT. Soldiers will therefore avoid the following associations and acts:

- Consensual contact or socializing (between or among Soldiers who are in BCT, OSUT or AIT) which involves handholding, embracing, caressing, kissing, touching, massaging or fondling of a sexual nature, engaging in sexual intercourse, or sodomy.
- Use of sexually explicit, suggestive, or obscene language or gestures directed towards, or with respect to another Soldier in BCT, OSUT or AIT.
- Gender-based or race-based harassment or disparaging language or actions (by a Soldier or a group of Soldiers in BCT, OSUT or AIT) directed towards another Soldier or group of Soldiers in BCT, OSUT or AIT.
- Entry into the living quarters, latrines, or other areas designated for the exclusive use of Soldiers of the opposite sex, unless required by training mission/ official duties or for health or safety emergencies.

However, language or socializing of a non-sexual, non-harassing nature between BCT, OSUT and AIT Soldiers is not illegal if the interaction is based on the esprit and enthusiasm generated by the basic training mission and the professional development associated with BCT, OSUT, and AIT.

Finally, there is no prohibition against Trainee Soldiers of the same or opposite sex talking to one another or developing friendships.

9-4. SHARP

A Soldier in the United States Army stands strong - a member of a band of brothers and sisters bound together by timeless values and sharing a sense of trust with and duty and loyalty to their fellow Soldiers that is unlike any other in the world.

Their willingness to sacrifice for each other, to never leave a fallen comrade, is what makes a Soldier strong - on the battlefield, and off.

When sexual harassment or sexual assault occurs, it is not only a direct violation of our Army Values and Warrior Ethos, but also an assault on what it means to serve in the Profession of Arms and the Army way of life - a life in which it is our duty to protect and take care of each other no matter the time, place, or circumstance. As a band of

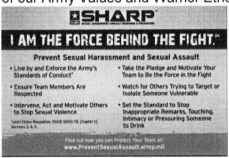

brothers and sisters, we have a personal and professional duty to intervene and prevent sexual harassment and sexual assault.

Sexual assault is a crime. It betrays victims and their Families; erodes the bedrock of trust upon which the Profession of Arms is grounded; and has a corrosive effect on our unit readiness, team cohesion, and command environment.

The damage resulting from sexual assault extends far beyond the victim, weakening the very health and morale of our Soldiers, breaking the bond of trust within our team, shattering the confidence Soldiers have in one another, and undermining unit readiness. Sexual assault can be prevented. As Soldiers, our Army Values demand that we act to stop these behaviors. There are no passive bystanders. Passive bystanders who do not assist, do not report, and do not try to help their fellow Soldiers as they see sexual harassment or sexual assaults occur are part of the problem. We must protect our team members. When we see or sense the risk of sexual harassment or sexual assault, we have a duty to intervene and protect our fellow Soldiers

At the Reception Battalion and during the initial phase of BCT and OSUT, Army leaders will provide you with information designed to inform, protect, and prevent you from  becoming a victim of sexual harassment and assault, and if you do become a victim, provide you with options for reporting the incident and getting help.

WHAT IS "I. A.M. STRONG"?

Intervene, Act, and Motivate (I. A.M.) STRONG is the Army's campaign to combat sexual harassment and sexual assault by engaging all Soldiers in preventing sexual assault before they occur.

INTERVENE   When I recognize a threat to my fellow Soldiers, I will have the personal courage to **INTERVENE** and prevent sexual assault. I will condemn acts of sexual harassment. I will not abide obscene gestures, language, or behavior. I am a Warrior and a member of a team. I will **INTERVENE**.

ACT You are my brother, my sister, my fellow Soldier. It is my duty to stand up for you, no matter the time or place. I will take **ACTION**. I will do what's right. I will prevent sexual harassment and sexual assault. I will not tolerate sexually offensive behavior. I will **ACT**.

MOTIVATE We are American Soldiers, **MOTIVATED** to keep our fellow Soldiers safe. It is our mission to prevent sexual harassment and sexual assault. We will denounce sexual misconduct. As Soldiers, we are all

MOTIVATED to take action. We are strongest...together

Sexual Harassment: Sexual harassment is a form of sex discrimination that involves unwelcome sexual advances, requests for sexual favors, and other verbal, or physical conduct of a sexual nature. The following conditions are signs of sexual harassment.

- Submission to such conduct is made either explicitly or implicitly a term or condition of a person's job, pay, or career, or
- Submission to, or rejection of, such conduct by a person is used as a basis for career or employment decisions affecting that person, or
- Such conduct has the purpose or effect of unreasonably interfering with an individual's work performance or creates an intimidating, hostile, or offensive working environment.

Note: "Workplace" is an expansive term for Soldiers and may include conduct on or off duty, 24 hours a day, on or off post.

Examples of Sexual Harassment:

Verbal:

- Making sexual jokes, gestures, remarks, or innuendos.
- Making comments about an individual's appearance, body, clothing, or sexual behavior.
- Spreading sexual rumors about an individual.
- Persistent, unwanted requests for social (dates) or sexual activity.
- Participating in sexually charged conversations.
- Nonverbal:
- Making and/or posting inappropriate sexual remarks to, or photos of, an Individual via social media sites, text message, or email.
- Displaying pornographic material or sexual photos in the workplace.
- Making a sexually offensive expression.
- Conduct of a sexual nature intended to embarrass, intimidate, demean, or degrade.

Physical Contact:

- Unwanted touching.

- Intimidation (blocking or cornering someone in a sexual way).

The Right response:

To determine if conduct falls under the category of sexual harassment, consider the following questions:

- Is the behavior sexual in nature?
- Is the behavior unwelcome?
- Does the behavior create a hostile or offensive work environment?
- Have sexual favors been demanded, requested, or suggested (especially as a condition of employment or career and job success)?
- **Your options:**
- Suggested individual actions to deal with sexual harassment include:
- Direct approach
- Indirect approach
- Third Party.
- Report harassment to the Chain of Command.
- File a formal Complaint.

- If you are uncomfortable because of certain sexual remarks or behaviors, you should be assertive. In responding to behavior that is or may become sexual harassment, you should tell the person how you feel.

- Describe what you do not like. Stay focused on the behavior and its impact. Clearly state what you want in the future. Tell any potential offender, "I do not want to hear that again" or, "Do not touch me again."

- If harassment continues after you have warned the harasser of their words and actions, go to your immediate superior unless that is the person doing the harassing.

In that case, go to their superior. If appropriate action is not taken, you may want to go up the chain of command to an Equal Opportunity Advisor/Equal Opportunity Representative or SHARP representatives such as the SARC or Victim Advocate (VA).

You can always tell a chaplain and ask for help.

Sexual Assault is an act intended to abuse, humiliate, harass, or degrade any person or to arouse or gratify the sexual desire of any person characterized by the use of force, threats, intimidation, or abuse of authority or when the victim does not or cannot consent.

The term includes a broad category of sexual offenses consisting of the following specific UCMJ offenses: rape, sexual assault, aggravated sexual contact, abusive sexual contact, forcible sodomy (forced oral or anal sex), or attempts to commit these offenses.

Sexual assault is a crime!

Examples of Sexual Assault may include:

- Rape and nonconsensual sodomy.
- Performing sexual acts or sexual contact with an individual who cannot give consent because he or she is sleeping/passed out or too impaired to consent due to alcohol or drugs and the condition is known or reasonably should have been known by the alleged offender. Using physical threats or force in order to engage in sexual contact with an individual.
- Performing sexual acts or sexual contact with an individual who has expressed lack of consent through words (e.g. said "no" or "stop") or through conduct.
- Sexual contact without permission, which can include fondling and hazing incidents.

Zero tolerance policy

The Army's policy states that sexual assault is a criminal offense incompatible with the Army's high standards of professionalism, discipline, and Army Values. Commanders and supervisors of perpetrators will take appropriate disciplinary action and/or administrative action.

Male and female Soldiers can commit rape.
The types of rape include physical and indirect force, date/acquaintance rape, and marital rape.
Your responsibility as a Soldier is to treat your fellow Soldiers the same as you would treat your buddy, or how you would prefer to be treated. This means if you see a Soldier in danger or trouble, you must take action.

What to do if you have been sexually assaulted

If you have been sexually assaulted or think you have been, go to a safe location away from the perpetrator.

If you want to talk with someone or want assistance, you have individuals who are ready to help. Make sure you understand the difference between a restricted and unrestricted report so that those you reach out to will understand your needs and can best assist you.

Restricted Report: Sexual assault victims who want to confidentially disclose a sexual assault without triggering an official investigation can contact a **SARC/SHARP Specialist/VA, or a healthcare provider**.

By filing a restricted report with these personnel, a victim can disclose the sexual assault without triggering an official investigation AND receive medical treatment, advocacy services, legal assistance, and counseling.

You can speak to a Chaplain and also maintain a restricted report. While a Chaplain cannot take a restricted report, Chaplains may not disclose privileged communication revealed in the practice of their ministry without the individual's informed consent. The Chaplain will report incidents of sexual assault to the SARC only with the victim's consent.

Unrestricted Report: This option is for victims of sexual assault who desire medical treatment, counseling, legal assistance, SARC/SHARP Specialist and VA assistance

and an official investigation of the crime.
When selecting unrestricted reporting, you may report the incident to the SARC/SHARP Specialist or VA, request healthcare providers to notify law enforcement, contact law enforcement yourself, or use current reporting channels, e.g., chain of command.

You can also call the DoD safe helpline at 877-995-5247 or your local installation helpline for further assistance.

Sex Rules
The Army has the following rules as both an awareness and reminder tool to keep you and your fellow Soldiers out of harm's way.

Rule No. 1: **Sexual assault is a crime.** Those in the Army found guilty of sexual assault could face a dishonorable discharge and up to 30 years in prison. *Integrity*. Do what's right, legally and morally.

Rule No. 2: **No always means no**. Unless the individual says yes, the answer is always no. *Loyalty*. Remain true to your fellow Soldiers.

Rule No. 3: **Without consent, it's sexual assault.** Never assume you have consent. Ask. *Honor.* Live up to the Army Values with every choice you make.

Rule No. 4: **Unwanted physical contact is wrong.** Unwanted or inappropriate touching, patting, tickling, pinching, bumping, hugging, grabbing, rubbing, etc. can be considered sexual assault. It's simple really. Keep your hands off! *Respect.* Treat others with dignity and respect.

Rule No. 5: **Sexually offensive remarks are sexual harassment.** Verbal sexual harassment includes telling sexual jokes, whistling in a sexually suggestive manner, and describing certain attributes of one's physical appearance in a sexual manner. *Duty.* Act in the best interest of your unit.

Rule No. 6: **Silence doesn't mean consent.** *Respect.* Clarify; ask before acting.

Rule No. 7: **Assess, discern and mitigate risk.** Recognizing the warning signs of a potential sexual assault can help assure that it never happens. *Selfless Service.* Ensure your Battle Buddy's safety.

Rule No. 8: **Set the Standard of Conduct**. Now that you're a Soldier, you are held to a higher standard of conduct. *Duty.* Be and hold others accountable.

Rule No. 9: **Stop sexual hazing, bullying and assault**. All acts of sexual harassment or assault break the bond of trust between battle buddies and weakens the unit.

Integrity. You are a Soldier, lead by example and stand up for what is right.

Rule No. 10: **Be a leader; not a passive bystander**. If you're ever in a situation where you witness someone sexually harassed or assaulted, it is your obligation to have the Personal Courage to intervene. *Personal Courage.* Intervene, Act and Motivate.

9-5. The Army Ethic

The Army Ethic, The Heart of the Army
The Army Ethic includes the moral principles that guide our decisions and actions as we fulfill our purpose to support and defend the Constitution and our way of life. Living the Army Ethic is the basis for our mutual trust with each other and the American people. Today our ethic is expressed in laws, values, and shared beliefs within American and Army cultures. The Army Ethic motivates our commitment as Soldiers and Army Civilians who are bound together to accomplish the Army mission as expressed in our historic and prophetic motto: **This We'll Defend.**

Living the Army Ethic inspires our shared identity as trusted Army professionals with distinctive roles as *honorable servants*, *Army experts*, and *stewards of the profession*. To honor these obligations we adopt, live by, and uphold the moral principles of the Army Ethic. Beginning with our solemn oath of service as defenders of the Nation, we voluntarily incur the extraordinary moral obligation to be trusted Army professionals.

Trusted Army professionals are

Honorable Servants of the Nation—Professionals of Character:

We serve honorably—according to the Army Ethic—under civilian authority while obeying the laws of the Nation and all legal orders; further, we reject and report illegal, unethical, or immoral orders or actions.

We take pride in honorably serving the Nation with integrity, demonstrating character in all aspects of our lives.

In war and peace, we recognize the intrinsic dignity and worth of all people, treating them with respect.

We lead by example and demonstrate courage by doing what is right despite risk, uncertainty, and fear; we candidly express our professional judgment to subordinates, peers, and superiors.

Army Experts—Competent Professionals:

We do our duty, leading and following with discipline, striving for excellence, putting the needs of others above our own, and accomplishing the mission as a team.

We accomplish the mission and understand it may demand courageously risking our lives and justly taking the lives of others.
We continuously advance the expertise of our chosen profession through life-long learning, professional development, and our certifications.

Stewards of the Army Profession—Committed Professionals:

We embrace and uphold the Army Values and standards of the profession, always accountable to each other and the American people for our decisions and actions.

We wisely use the resources entrusted to us, ensuring our Army is well led and well prepared, while caring for Soldiers, Army Civilians, and Families.

We continuously strengthen the essential characteristics of the Army Profession, reinforcing our bond of trust with each other and the American people.

Army Values within the Moral Principles of the Army Ethic

Integrity: "Do what is right* legally and morally."
Decisions & actions are consistent with the moral principles of the Army Ethic.

We take pride in honorably serving the Nation with integrity, demonstrating character in all aspects of our lives.
We embrace and uphold the Army Values and standards of the profession, always accountable to each other and the American people for our decisions and actions.

Duty: "Fulfill your obligations. Accept responsibility for your own actions and those entrusted to your care." **Contribute your best effort to accomplish the mission; do what is right* to the best of your ability; strive for excellence in all endeavors.**
We do our duty, leading and following with discipline, striving for excellence, putting the needs of others above our own, and accomplishing the mission as a team.
We continuously advance the expertise of our chosen profession through life-long learning, professional development, and our certifications.

Honor: "Live up to all the Army Values." **Show reverence for truth and justice, have due regard for property, and commit to uphold the Army Ethic.**
Seek to discover the truth, decide what is right (ethical, effective, and efficient), and demonstrate the character, competence, and commitment to act accordingly.
[Expectations for Army Professionals - ADRP 1, para 2-29]

Loyalty: "Bear true faith and allegiance to the U.S. Constitution, the Army, your unit, and other Soldiers."
Bear true faith and allegiance to the U.S. Constitution.
We serve honorably—according to the Army Ethic—under civilian authority while obeying the laws of the Nation and all legal orders; further, we reject and report illegal, unethical, or immoral orders or actions.

[Selfless] **Service**: "Put the welfare of the nation, the Army, and your subordinates before your own."
Contribute to the well-being and benefit of others; teamwork.

We continuously strengthen the essential characteristics of the Army Profession, reinforcing our bond of trust with each other and the American people.
We wisely use the resources entrusted to us, ensuring our Army is well led and well prepared, while caring for Soldiers, Army Civilians, and Families.

Respect: "Treat people as they should be treated."
Recognize the intrinsic dignity and worth of all people.
In war and peace, we recognize the intrinsic dignity and worth of all people, treating them with respect.

[Personal] **Courage**: "Our ability to face fear, danger, or adversity, both physical and moral courage." **Resolve to do what is right (duty) despite risk, uncertainty, and fear.**

We accomplish the mission and understand it may demand courageously risking our lives and justly taking the lives of others. We lead by example and demonstrate courage by doing what is right despite risk, uncertainty, and fear; we candidly express our professional judgment to subordinates, peers, and superiors.

* right = ethical, effective, and efficient.

9-6. Standards and Principles of Ethical Conduct

You are now part of a culture that lives up to a higher standard. As a Soldier, you are also a member of the Executive Branch of the U.S. government. Your actions must uphold the letter and the spirit of US laws and regulations governing ethical conduct. The President has issued Executive Order 12731, known as the "14 General Principles of Ethical Conduct" These principles summarize the ethics laws and regulations all Soldiers must follow:

(1) Public service is a public trust, requiring Soldiers to place loyalty to the Constitution, the laws and ethical principles above any private gain.

(2) Soldiers will not hold financial interests that would conflict with the conscientious performance of their duty.
(3) Soldiers will not engage in financial transactions using Government information that isn't available to the general public, or allow the improper use of such information to further any private interest.

(4) All Soldiers will not, except as permitted by the Standards of Ethical Conduct, solicit or accept any gift or other item of monetary value from any person or entity seeking official action from, doing business with, or conducting activities regulated by the Army, or whose interests may be substantially affected by the performance or nonperformance of the Soldier's duties.

(5) Soldiers will always put forth honest effort in the performance of their duties.

(6) Soldiers will not knowingly make unauthorized commitments or promises of any kind appearing to bind the Government.

(7) Soldiers will not use their public office for private gain.

(8) Soldiers will act impartially and not give preferential treatment to any private organization or individual.

(9) Soldiers will protect and conserve Federal property and will not use it for other than authorized activities.

(10) Soldiers will not engage in outside employment or activities, including seeking or negotiating for employment, that conflict with official Government duties and responsibilities.

(11) Soldiers will disclose waste, fraud, abuse, and corruption to appropriate authorities.

(12) Soldiers will satisfy in good faith their obligations as citizens, including all financial obligations, especially those -- such as Federal, State, or local taxes -- that are imposed by law.

(13) Soldiers will adhere to all laws and regulations that provide equal opportunity for all Americans regardless of race, color, religion, sex, national origin, age, or handicap.

(14) Soldiers will avoid any actions creating the appearance that they are violating the law or the ethical standards set forth in the Standards of Ethical Conduct.

If you are ever confused as to what these requirements of ethical conduct mean, there are online and local resources to help make the right ethical decisions. One way to do that is to go to the Army's Office of General Counsel website at: http://ogc.hqda.pentagon.mil/ and click "ethics" link. http://ogc.hqda.pentagon.mil/ and click "ethics" link. Your base legal office has an ethics counselor for advice, or TRADOC Ethics Counselor at (757) 501-5757 or 5659.

Chapter 10 – Reference Material

10-1. The National Anthem

Written by Francis Scott Key in 1814, the Star Spangled Banner was played at military occasions ordered by President Woodrow Wilson in 1916, and in 1931 was designated as our national anthem by an Act of Congress.

The Star Spangled Banner is the timeless rendition of our sacred American Flag and country's patriotic spirit.

The Star Spangled Banner

Oh, say, can you see, by the dawn's early light,

What so proudly we hailed at the twilight's last gleaming?

Whose broad stripes and bright stars, thro' the perilous fight'

O'er the ramparts we watched were so gallantly streaming.

And the rockets' red glare, the bombs bursting in air,

Gave proof through the night that our flag was still there.

Oh, say, does that Star-Spangled Banner yet wave

O'er the land of the free and the home of the brave?

10-2. The Army Song

The Army Song tells the heroic story of our past, present, and future. It was originally written by First Lieutenant Edmund L. Gruber, a Field Artillery officer, in 1908 and it was adopted in 1952 as the official song of our Army. As a time-honored tradition, the song is played at the conclusion of every U.S. Army ceremony in which all Soldiers are expected to stand and proudly sing the lyrics.

Army Song

March along, sing our song, with the Army of the free.

Count the brave, count the true, who have fought to victory.
We're the Army and proud of our name!
We're the Army and proudly proclaim.

First to fight for the right, And to build the Nation's might,
And The Army Goes Rolling Along.
Proud of all we have done, Fighting till the battle's won,
And the Army Goes Rolling Along.

Then it's Hi! Hi! Hey! The Army's on its way.
Count off the cadence loud and strong.
For where e'er we go, you will always know,
That The Army Goes Rolling Along.

10-3. The Code of Conduct

I. I am an American, fighting in the forces which guard my country and our way of life. I am prepared to give my life in their defense.

II. I will never surrender of my own free will. If in command, I will never surrender the members of my command while they still have the means to resist.

III. If I am captured, I will continue to resist by all means available. I will make every effort to escape and aid others to escape. I will accept neither parole nor special favors from the enemy.

IV. If I become a prisoner of war, I will keep faith with my fellow prisoners. I will give no information or take part in any action, which might be harmful to my comrades. If I am senior, I will take command. If not, I will obey the lawful orders of those appointed over me and will back them up in every way.

V. When questioned, should I become a prisoner of war, I am required to give name, rank, service number, and date of birth. I will evade answering further questions to the utmost of my ability. I will make no oral or written statements disloyal to my country and its allies or harmful to their cause.

VI. I will never forget that I am an American, fighting for freedom, responsible for my actions, and dedicated to the principles which made my country free. I will trust in my God and in the United States of America.

The Code of Conduct is our guide for how all Soldiers, Sailors, Airmen and Marines must conduct themselves if captured by the enemy. The Code of Conduct, in six brief Articles, addresses the intense situations and decisions that, to some degree, all military service members could encounter. It contains the critical information for U.S. prisoners of war to survive honorably while faithfully resisting the enemy's efforts of exploitation.

10-4. General Orders/Special Orders

General Orders:

1. I will guard everything within the limits of my post and quit my post only when properly relieved.
2. I will obey my special orders and perform all my duties in a military manner.
3. I will report violations of my special orders, emergencies, and anything not covered in my instructions to the commander of relief.

BCT / OSUT / AIT Special Orders:
Additional requirements or instructions imbedded within the general orders.

1. I will not do anything that would injure, degrade or harm my teammates...for I am an American Soldier sworn to defend the Values that we hold dear as a nation.
2. I will not go anywhere without my battle buddy, and will take action to protect him/her from harm, whether that harm is to them self or at the hands of others...for I am the first line of defense in the protection of my teammates.
3. I trust my comrades with my life, but if I observe any threats against my battle buddy or my

teammates, it is my personal responsibility to report that infraction to my leadership...for it is my duty as a Soldier to serve and protect others.

10-5. Guard duty

One of the most important duties you will perform in the Army is guard duty. In a combat zone or unit area, cautious guards can mean the difference between life and death. However, guards are important everywhere due to the terrorist threats that can occur anywhere. Knowing your General Orders and Initial Military Training Special Orders, as mentioned earlier in this book, will have a major impact during Guard Duty.

Reacting to an Inspecting Officer

When you are on guard duty and approached by an inspecting officer, these steps are followed:
- Stop walking and assume the position of attention.
- When the inspecting officer approaches, render a proper hand salute.
- When the salute is returned, execute order arms.
- Remain at attention.
- The inspecting officer will command, "At ease."

- The inspecting officer may ask questions pertaining to your general orders, special orders, and what has transpired at your post.
- When finished with the inspection, the inspecting officer will say, "Carry on."
- Assume the position of attention and render a proper hand salute, holding it until it is returned.
- Resume walking your post.

Challenging unknown persons

The following steps are carried out when challenging unknown persons (night) and summoning the commander of the relief:

- Upon seeing or hearing an unknown person, come to port arms.
- Issue the command "Halt." (Person halts.)
- Call out "Who is/goes there?" Unknown person identifies him/herself.
- State "Advance to be recognized."
- Command "Halt," when the person can be seen but not closer than 2 to 3 meters away.
- Say "State your business." Unknown person states reason for presence in guarded area.

- Require the unknown person to place their identification on the ground and move back six steps.
- Check the identification while keeping the person under observation.
- If the identification (ID) and authorization do not match, move to the phone and call the commander of the relief while keeping the person under observation.
- Release the person to the commander of the relief and explain that their identification and authorization do not match.

10-6. Army Organizations

Active Army and Reserve Component

The U.S. Army consists of the Active Army, the ARNG and the USAR.

Army unit organizations

The squad/section is the smallest unit, consisting of eight to ten Soldiers. <u>You will be assigned to a squad or a section when you report to your first unit.</u>

The platoon includes the Platoon leader, Platoon Sergeant, and two or more squads. (Normally 4 squads)

The company includes the company commander, first sergeant, and two or more platoons. (Normally 3 to 4 squads)

The battalion includes the battalion commander, his or her staff and headquarters, the command sergeant major, and approximately 3-5 companies.

The brigade consists of two to five battalions. It includes the brigade commander, command sergeant major, and a headquarters.

Chapter 11 – First Duty Station

11-1. Where Will I Serve?

Our Army has Soldiers and units in every State, Commonwealth and Possession across the United States. If you are in the active component, you may find yourself stationed in Alaska, Hawaii, Japan, Germany, Korea, Italy, and Turkey. Our presence is needed around the world to defend citizens, preserve liberties, and fight for freedom.

If your unit has been designated to deploy to perform regional missions, the unit will prepare you for that deployment.

11-2. How can I prepare?

The training you are receiving now is preparing you for the challenges you will meet in your first unit, as you join a new team, and establish a new group of "battle buddies."

Your first assignment will be even more challenging and even more rewarding than your BCT / OSUT / AIT experience, but only if you prepare yourself mentally for the journey. Have confidence and trust in your unit leaders that they will provide you with the knowledge, training, and physical preparation for that next gate in your professional development.

11-3. Promotions

Progressing through the enlisted Army ranks is a major accomplishment. In the performance of your military duties, opportunities for education and self-development are available. This provides you with enhanced skills and allows your leaders to assess your leadership potential. Opportunities for advancement are available for you if you are committed to pursuing these opportunities.

There are two ways to get promoted to Specialist:

One is automatic as long as you have no punitive actions with the following time in grade (TIG) [the amount of time you have served continuously on the rank/grade] and service (TIS) [the amount of time you have served in the Army]:

Promotion	Time in Service (TIS)	Time in Grade (TIG)
PVT - PV2	6 months	N/A
PV2 - PFC	12 months	4 months
PFC - SPC	24 months	6 months

The other is to receive a waiver from the Commander. The numbers available are few and depend on the Army's need for that specific rank. A waiver can be used to wave either TIS or TIG, but not both. The Commander will pick the best Soldiers per rank to receive the waivers allocated each month. With a waiver, minimum promotion requirements are:

Promotion	Time in Service (TIS)	Time in Grade (TIG)
PVT - PV2	4 months	N/A
PV2 - PFC	6 months	2 months
PFC - SPC	18 months	3 months

To get promoted to Sergeant, Specialists must meet the minimum TIS and TIG to be eligible and then must appear before a unit promotion board (battalion or higher) and be selected for promotion.

Once the board selects you for promotion, then your promotion points are calculated. The Army assesses every month how many Sergeants they need in your MOS. If the points drop below your number, you will be selected for promotion. The number varies from month to month.

Promotions points are earned through merits (awards and certificates), schooling (both Military and civilian education), and Soldier proficiency scores (APFT and Weapons Qualification). Minimum TIS and TIG requirements are:

Promotion SPC - SGT	Time in Service (TIS)	Time in Grade (TIG)
Primary Zone	35 months	7 months
Secondary Zone	17 months	5 months

To excel as an Army Professional, every Soldier should set goals. Determine what you want from this opportunity to serve and continue the journey that you have embarked.

Depending on the MOS and length of your contract, it is possible to make Specialist or Sergeant during your first enlistment. Whether you leave the Army at the conclusion of your enlistment or continue serving, your accomplishments will define who you are and inspire you to excel in and out of the military.

Examples of goal-setting during your first enlistment:

- Become proficient on every weapon system within your platoon
- Become licensed to drive every vehicle within your company
- Strive to obtain high individual scores on weapons and physical training
- Volunteer to attend resident military schools and courses when they become available in your MOS
- Work on your civilian education with a goal to receive an associate or higher degree before the end of your enlistment
- Represent your unit and compete for Soldier of the month selection

You can learn more about promotions through your NCO support channel. You can track your career path through the Army Career Tracker at: https://actnow.army.mil/

11-4. Total Army Sponsorship Program (TASP) and Army Career Tracker (ACT)

Total Army Sponsorship Program (TASP)

Information about the Total Army Sponsorship Program is available at https://actnow.army.mil. A Common Access Card (CAC) or DS LOGON is required to access ACT. Click on the Sponsorship Help menu item, then click on General Information, Active component, or Reserve TPU. To begin, log on to ACT and review your Assignment Instruction Message. Open and read the Welcome Letter in order to learn information about your new assignment and the Sponsor who will be guiding you through your transition to a new unit. Many steps must occur in order to ensure a smooth transition for a PCSing individual, or Incoming Soldier, to his or her new unit or location. It is your responsibility to complete sections 1, 2, 4, and 5 of DA Form 5434. In Section 1, make sure that your information is correct, and then confirm that you have been counseled on the Total Army Sponsorship Program by clicking the checkbox. In Section 2, fill out your personal contact information and

Family details. In Section 4, complete the information about your losing unit. In Section 5, fill out any additional Family considerations that must be taken into account during your transition to a new unit. When you are done, click SAVE.

You are linked to a Sponsor through ACT and will receive a welcome message from him or her. You then receive information about your Sponsor as well as a prompt to begin completing DA Form 5434. Your Sponsor and Sponsorship Coordinators are notified if the form is not completed. To view the completed DA Form 5434, navigate to the Sponsorship primary navigation option, and choose COORDINATOR DASHBOARD from the secondary navigation drop down. Click on the DA FORM 5434 THERMOMETER DETAIL view, and choose your name to view your form. You will receive a notification in your Messages icon if your Sponsor is changed or removed for any reason. Additionally, all PCSing Soldiers are required to complete both in-processing and out-processing surveys for their gaining and losing units, respectively. Underneath the Sponsorship option in the primary navigation column, choose SURVEYS from the secondary navigation drop down. Complete the survey and submit.

Army Career Tracker:

(ACT) is a leadership development tool that integrates training and education into one personalized, easy-to-use website. Users can search multiple education and training resources, monitor their career development and receive personalized advice from their leadership.

Soldiers are encouraged to access ACT at least monthly to communicate with their leaders, supervisors, and mentors about career development goals; to and obtain the latest news and information tailored to their career program and individual needs. Users are also expected to use ACT to create and track their personal and professional career development goals. Users can search multiple education and training resources, monitor their career development and receive personalized advice from their leaders.

The system allows supervisors and mentors to monitor their employees' goals and provide them developmental recommendations, notifications and career advice. Supervisors will be able to view records for both their Civilian and military employees

11-5. Soldier for Life Program

The U.S. Army established Soldier for Life in July 2012 to maintain trust with our Army Family during and after service. This program is designed to enable Soldiers, Retired Soldiers, Veterans, and Families to leave military service "Career Ready", and connect to an established network to find employment, education, and health resources. It focuses on the current serving population to instill the Soldier for Life mindset of service.

Soldier for Life- Transition Assistance Program promotes lifelong learning, individual development, and transition-related requirements throughout a Soldier's military Career. This program combines employment and education workshops and seminars tailored to prepare and connect transitioning Soldiers to meaningful civilian employment and education opportunities.

Soldier for Life Centers- Centers are located on installations, Posts, camps and stations where Soldiers and Families can find resources to assist them in making educated decisions and sound plans during all phases of their military lives: in-service, and post transition.

The Soldier's for Life goal is to "Start Strong, Serve Strong, and Continue Strong"

Once a Soldier, Always a Soldier.....a Soldier for Life!

Appendix A – Army Resources
A-1. Leave and Earnings Statement

DEFENSE FINANCE AND ACCOUNTING SERVICE MILITARY LEAVE AND EARNINGS STATEMENT									
ID	NAME (Last, First, MI)	SOC. SEC. NO.	GRADE E5	PAY DATE 040211	YRS SVC 04	ETS 100210	BRANCH AF	ADSN/DSSN	PERIOD COVERED 1-31 JUL 08

ENTITLEMENTS		DEDUCTIONS		ALLOTMENTS		SUMMARY	
Type	Amount	Type	Amount	Type	Amount	+Amt Fwd	.00
A BASE PAY	2247.30	FEDERAL TAXES	88.46	DISCRETIONARY ALT	1521.00	+Tot Ent	4266.73
B BAS	294.43	FICA-SOC SECURITY	139.33	TRICARE DENTAL	11.58	-Tot Ded	1570.22
C BAH	1725.00	FICA-MEDICARE	32.59			-Tot Alt	1532.58
D		SGLI	27.00			=Net Amt	1163.93
E		AFRH	.50			-Cr Fwd	.00
F		FAMILY SGLI	5.50			=EOM Pay	1163.93
G		TSP	112.37				
H		MID-MONTH-PAY	1164.47				
I							
J							
K							
L							
M							
N							
O						DIEMS 040211	RETPLAN CHOICE
TOTAL	4266.73		1570.22		1532.58		

LEAVE	BF Bal 25.5	Ernd 25.0	Used 11	Cr Bal 39.5	ETS Bal 85.5	Lv Lost .0	Lv Paid .0	Use/Lose .0	FED TAXES	Wage Period 2134.93	Wage YTD 13682.36	M/S M	Ex 02	Add'l Tax .00	Tax YTD 493.01
FICA TAXES	Wage Period 2247.30		Soc Wage YTD 14402.50		Soc Tax YTD 892.94		Med Wage YTD 14402.50		Med Tax YTD 208.83	STATE TAXES	St AK	Wage Period .00	Wage YTD .00	M/S N	Ex 00	Tax YTD .00
PAY DATA	BAQ Type W/DEP	BAQ Depn SPOUSE	VHA Zip 08641	Rent Amt .00	Share 1	Stat R	JFTR	Depns 0	2D JFTR	BAS Type	Charity YTD .00	TPC	PACIDN		
THRIFT SAVINGS PLAN (TSP)	Base Pay Rate 5	Base Pay Current .00	Spec Pay Rate 0	Spec Pay Current .00	Inc Pay Current 0	Inc Pay Current .00	Bonus Pay Rate 0	Bonus Pay Current .00							
		TSP YTD Deductions 720.14			Deferred 720.14			Exempt .00							

REMARKS: YTD ENTITLE 27768.11   YTD DEDUCT 2557.92

IF TSP ELECTION AMT EXCEEDS NET AMT
DUE, TSP WILL NOT BE DEDUCTED.
-LEAVE CARRYOVER INCREASED TO 75 DAYS FOR
FY08. NO ACTION REQUIRED BY MEMBERS. DFAS
WILL BEGIN RESTORING AFTER 1 OCT 08.
-MYPAY HAS ALLOWED MBRS TO ELECT A HARD-
COPY LES VIA US MAIL. AF POLICY IS TO
PROVIDE AN ELECTRONIC LES. EFF 1 OCT (SEP
LES), AF WILL NO LONGER PRINT LES STATEMENTS
IF AVAILABLE ON MYPAY. THANK YOU FOR YOUR
SUPPORT.
-IF YOUR SPOUSE WANTS INFO ABOUT THE MILITARY
LIFESTYLE WE INVITE HIM/HER TO JOIN US FOR
THE NEXT HEART LINK SPOUSES ORIENTATION.
LUNCH AND CHILD CARE ARE PROVIDED. CALL YOUR

BASE AIRMAN & FAMILY READINESS CTR FOR
DETAILS.
-IF YOU GAMBLE WITH SAFETY...YOU BET YOUR
LIFE.
-ELECTIONS ARE COMING! UPDATE YOUR ADDRESS
TO GET AN ABSENTEE BALLOT. REQUEST YOUR
BALLOT FOR THE PRESIDENTIAL AND STATE
ELECTIONS. SEE YOUR VOTING ASST. OFFICER
OR WWW.FVAP.GOV.
    TSP   080701(183)
    RATE CHG SGLI   080701(183)
    CHANGE GRADE   080701(184)
    BAH BASED ON W/DEP, ZIP 08641
    BANK
    ACCT #

WWW.DFAS.MIL

DFAS Form 702, Jan 02

The leave and earning statement (LES) is your detailed pay statement, which is issued at the end of each month. It shows your entitlements, deductions, and allotments, and it provides a summary of all pay transactions. It also shows your end-of-month pay and where your pay is being deposited. It is your duty to review the LES and ensure the information is correct. If you find an error, report it to your chain of command immediately.

1. ID/Administration. The first section is the ID/Administration section. It shows your name, social security number (SSN), pay grade, pay date, years of service, ETS date, your branch of service, the code number of your servicing finance office, and the period covered by the LES.

2. Entitlements. The second section is the entitlements section and lists all of your pay and allowances. Some common entries in this section include:

- Base Pay: Soldiers base pay is taxable and is calculated according to pay grade and years of service.

- Allowances: Soldiers are entitled to non-taxable allowances in addition to monthly base pay.

- Basic Allowance for Subsistence (BAS). BAS is tax-free money the Army pays Soldiers who are

not relying on Dining Facilities (DFACs) for all their meals (i.e., married Soldiers).
- Basic Allowance for Housing (BAH) is tax-free money the Army pays Soldiers for housing.
- Clothing Allowance (CA). Active duty enlisted Soldiers are paid a tax free Clothing Allowance to defray the cost of maintaining uniforms and replacing worn-out uniforms.

3. Deductions. There may be several deductions taken out of Soldier's pay, such as taxes and fines.

4. Allotments. There are various types of allotments and limits as to the number of allotments Soldiers may have at one time.

5. Summary. Provides the dollar totals of various sections and of your LES.

6. Leave. Shows a running balance and a history of your leave account.

7. Federal Tax Section. Federal taxes are figured on your pay.

8. FICA Section. Federal Insurance Contributions Act (FICA) taxes are figured on your taxable pay. FICA data is shown in the first five blocks.

9. State Tax. (Similar to Federal tax block)

10. Pay Data. DFAS uses the "PAY DATA" section for information about entitlements that relate to your pay account.

11. Thrift Savings Plan (TSP). This section shows information pertaining to your Thrift Savings Plan. The TSP is a program available to you, which invests a portion of your pay into a variety of available funds

12. Remarks. This section shows your entitlements and deductions so far this calendar year. Other than that, the "REMARKS" section explains entries in the other sections, as well as other useful information.

A-2. Managing personal finances

It is your duty as a Soldier to fulfill all of your financial obligations and provide for your Family members. There are several key components to achieving this task. Take action to ensure you are receiving your paycheck and have financial systems in place to meet your needs. Inquire with other individuals about the services they receive and make educated financial decisions.

MyPay: Soldiers can review and print their leave and earnings statement, thrift savings plan investments, savings deposit program Statement, allotments, savings bonds purchases, and direct deposit amounts at https://mypay.dfas.mil/mypay.aspx.Ensure you visit the official military web site only.

Sure-Pay program: The Army requires all Soldiers to enroll in the sure-pay program. This means that you must have your paycheck deposited directly to a checking or savings account. If you close or change this account, you must ensure that you go to MyPay and update account information.

The Army will pay you once per month on the first of each month, or twice per month on the 1st and the 15th - your choice based on your budget requirements.

You must carefully review your monthly leave and earning statement to ensure that your pay is being deposited properly and you are receiving all of the benefits (Base Pay, Basic Allowance for Housing (BAH), etc.) that you are entitled.

Bank deposit account: There are some key items to consider when choosing the financial institution at which you will keep your direct deposit account.

First, inquire if there is a monthly service charge for maintaining a checking account. Numerous institutions offer free checking, as long as you have set up Sure-Pay.

Inquire if there a charge for using ATMs. Cash withdrawal charges can be expensive, and often banks do not charge ATM fees at local branches, or refund fees from other banks.

Third, as the Army requires frequent moves, it is important to consider a bank that provides service at numerous military installations or online where you could be stationed.

Service Members Civil Relief Act (SCRA): The SCRA offers many benefits and protections to Soldiers and their Families. It allows a service member to postpone or suspend certain civil actions while mobilized or deployed for active duty, including evictions, mortgage foreclosures, bankruptcies and other civil lawsuits. It covers all military service members from the date they enter active duty through 30 to 90 days after active duty discharge. The SCRA also offers protection against high interest rate debt secured prior to entry into Active Duty; capping interest rates on qualifying debt at 6%. Ensure you call all debtors (credit cards, car loans, personal loans, etc.) as soon as possible and notify them of your service, and that the SCRA should apply to your debt. Failure to comply can result in legal action.

Military Lending Act: The Military Lending Act limits the annual percentage rate for credit to no more than 36 percent and includes associated costs of the loan, like fees and the sale of credit products sold with the loan. This rate is known as the military annual percentage rate, or MAPR. Additionally, the Military Lending Act prohibits mandatory arbitration, difficult contract provisions, using an allotment to secure the loan, waiving Servicemembers Civil Relief Act rights, charging a penalty for early payments, using a post-dated check to secure a loan, refinancing certain loans and the use of bank accounts and car titles to secure certain other loans. Current protections cover payday, vehicle title and tax refund anticipation loans. Purchases made through rent-to-own and overdrafts on checking accounts are not covered.

Lastly, while a local bank may be your best option, you may have to change accounts when you make a permanent change of station move.

Check writing: You must pay close attention to each transaction to ensure you always know your checking account balance; this ensures you have sufficient funds in the account and do not write a fraudulent check.

There are several consequences for writing a bad check, service charges, negative credit ratings, and additional punishments if the check was used on post.

Retirement: Although retirement may seem a long way off, the sooner you start saving the better off you will be.

A delay of only 5 years in starting contributions could mean several hundred thousand dollars later!

The Army's retirement contribution system is the Thrift Savings Plan (TSP). TSP contributions can be started on MyPay and managed at: https://www.tsp.gov. In most cases for new Soldiers the ROTH option (paying taxes upfront but no taxes on interest when the money is withdrawn) is better, but it is important to research all options and talk to the financial planner at your Soldier Support Center.

Military One Source: http://www.militaryonesource.mil/financial-and-legal and many other resources are available online to help you determine how much to save, and how much money will be needed in retirement.

The DoD Blended Retirement System is going live on 1 January, 2018. Below is a graphic covering a quick overview of the current and new systems.

The U.S. Uniformed Services Blended Retirement System | *At a Glance*

Saving with the New Blended Retirement System

The Fiscal Year 2016 National Defense Authorization Act provides our military force with a modernized retirement plan built for retirement savings. Beginning in 2018, our service members can get **automatic and matching Thrift Savings Plan contributions** as well as mid-career **compensation incentives** in addition to monthly **annuities for life**. All service members under the current system are grandfathered into today's retirement system.

Today's Retirement System:

Annuity

2.5% x Years Served x Retired Pay Base
after completing 20 years of service

❶ Automatic and Matching Contributions
Automatic contributions are seen immediately

Your Contribution	DoD Auto Contribution	DoD Matches	Total
0%	1%	0%	1%
1%	1%	1%	3%
2%	1%	2%	5%
3%	1%	3%	7%
4%	1%	3.5%	8.5%
5%	1%	4%	10%

The DoD automatically contributes **1%** of your basic pay to your **Thrift Savings Plan** after **60 days of service**.

You'll see matching contributions at the start of 3 through the completion of 26 years of service, and...

You're fully vested—it's yours to keep—as of the beginning of 3 years of service and goes with you when you leave.

❷ Continuation Pay
Received at the mid-career point

You may receive a **cash payment** in exchange for additional service.

❸ Full Retired Pay Annuity
Received after completing 20 years of service

2% x Years Served = Retired Pay Base

Calculate your **retired pay base** by **averaging the highest 36 months of basic pay**. You'll gain this monthly annuity for life after completing 20 years of service.

Options for Collecting Your Retired Pay

Active Component
Full retired pay annuity

Reserve Component
Full retired pay annuity beginning at age 60*

or

Lump sum with reduced retired pay
50% or 25% of monthly retired pay annuity bumps back up to 100% at full retirement age (67 in most cases)

*Could be earlier based on creditable active service

Effective Date of the New System

Your Retirement System
If you joined the service...

▸ **After December 31, 2017**
You'll be automatically enrolled in the Blended Retirement System.

▸ **After December 31, 2005 but before January 1, 2018**
You'll have the choice to enroll in the Blended Retirement System or remain in today's current retirement system.

▸ **Before January 1, 2006**
You'll be grandfathered and remain in today's current retirement system.

Additional information coming soon.
Sources: Sections 631, 632, 633, 634, and 635 of the Fiscal Year 2016 National Defense Authorization Act.

A-3. Tri-Service Health Care (TRICARE)

The Army is dedicated to taking care of its most important assets, Soldiers and military Family members.

TRICARE is the Department of Defense's worldwide health care program available to eligible beneficiaries from the uniformed services.

TRICARE is free to Soldiers but may involve some out-of-pocket expenses for Family members. The cost varies depending on the Soldier's rank and the specific TRICARE program option in which the Family member is enrolled.

Through the TRICARE program, Family members can also go to civilian health care providers if they desire. But before going to a civilian practitioner, Family members should talk to the Beneficiary Counseling and Assistance Coordinator (BCAC) at the nearest military health care facility to see if there are any out-of-pocket expenses. The BCAC will confirm your registration in the Defense Enrollment Eligibility Reporting System (DEERS), and can provide a list of doctors in your local area who will accept TRICARE patients.

When permitted, visit TRICARE online for more information on your military health benefits and regional health plans—*www.tricare.mil*.

A-4. Servicemembers' Group Life Insurance (SGLI)

As a United States Soldier, you may encounter hostile situations while stationed abroad and in combat. The well-being of your Family is of the greatest concern to the Army.

One of the many benefits afforded Soldiers is the opportunity to purchase very low-cost life insurance. SGLI provides up to a maximum of $400,000. SGLI automatically covers you for this maximum amount unless you select in writing a lesser amount, in increments of $50,000. You may also decline SGLI altogether, but this decision is so important that you must also do that in writing. The payment is deducted automatically from your pay each month. Soldiers with Families almost always select coverage in the maximum amount.

Spouses and children are eligible for Family SGLI. Coverage for a spouse is automatically $100,000 unless a lesser amount, in steps of $10,000, is chosen.

When permitted, visit the Service member's Life Insurance website maintained by the Department of Veterans Affairs for additional information and assistance with enrollment—
http://www.benefits.va.gov/insurance/sgli.asp#cover

A-5. Dental

The level of dental care will vary from post to post, but it is available for all Soldiers. Family member care is generally not available at military dental facilities.

Family members may get dental insurance through the TRICARE Dental Program (TDP). The TDP is dental insurance in which you pay a monthly fee in exchange for Family coverage. It is a voluntary, cost effective, comprehensive program offered worldwide by the Department of Defense to Family members of all active duty branches of the military, Selected Reserve, and Individual Ready Reserve members and their Family members.

Just as is the case for TRICARE health care, Family members must be registered in DEERS to be eligible for the TRICARE Dental Program.

In order to participate, the Soldier must have 12 months left on his or her service commitment at the time of enrollment, and submit an enrollment form with the first month's premium or enroll online using a charge card. The monthly premiums will usually be deducted from the Soldier's pay, although there are other payment options.

Depending on the dental procedures performed, treatment may be completely covered by the insurance, or there may be co-payments required.

There is a maximum annual amount that TRICARE will pay for any one beneficiary. Once that yearly amount is reached for the individual, all costs above the maximum must be paid for by the Family.

When permitted, complete information and instructions on how to enroll and find a local dental provider are available on-line at:
http://www.tricare.mil/CoveredServices/Dental.aspx.

A-6. Army Emergency Relief

Army Emergency Relief (AER) is a private nonprofit organization incorporated in 1942 by the Secretary of War and the Army Chief of Staff. AER's mission is to provide emergency financial assistance to Soldiers and their Families.

What can AER do?

Help with emergency financial needs for:

- Food, rent or utilities
- Emergency transportation and vehicle repair
- Funeral expenses
- Medical/dental expenses

- Provide college scholarships to children, spouses, and surviving spouses of Soldiers.
- Additional Benefits:
    - Lifetime membership in the Army Air Force Mutual Aid Association for surviving Families of Soldiers who die on active duty.
    - Grants for wounded Soldiers medically evacuated from a theater of combat
    - Personal Financial Management Training for Soldiers in AIT

Who is eligible?

- Active duty Soldiers, single or married, and their Family members.
- Army National Guard and Army Reserve Soldiers on continuous active duty for more than 30 days and their Family members (Title 10, USC).
- Soldiers retired from active duty for longevity or physical disability, and their Family members.
- Army National Guard and Army Reserve Soldiers who retired at age 60, and their Family members.
- Surviving spouses and orphans of Soldiers who died while on active duty or after they retired.

How do I get assistance?

- Through your unit chain of command and the installation AER section.
- If there is no AER section near you, you can get assistance through:
  - American Red Cross (local chapter, or 24 hour emergency services)
  - Air Force Base (Air Force Aid Society)
  - Navy/Marine Corps Base (Navy-Marine Corps Relief Society)
  - Coast Guard Base (Coast Guard Mutual Assistance)

Can my spouse get AER help if I'm away?

Yes. Your spouse should bring:
- Power of Attorney
- Military ID Card
- Substantiating documents

What kind of assistance can I expect?
- An interest free loan.
- A grant if repayment of loan will cause undue hardship.
- Part loan and part grant.

How can I help AER?

- Remind fellow Soldiers about AER when they have financial emergencies.
- Support AER with a contribution and encourage others to contribute.
- The Army-wide annual AER fund campaign is conducted 1 March –15 May.
- You can contribute to your local AER fund campaign or send your contribution to AER National Headquarters.
- All contributions are tax deductible.
- Unsolicited donations are accepted any time by mail or on-line.

For more information contact your local AER officer or visit our website at www.aerhq.org.

A-7. Soldier for Life and Credentialing

If you serve faithfully and honorably, **you are a Soldier for Life**, whether you are in the active or reserve components, or serve for one enlistment or a long career.

The Army wants to be a partner in your lifelong success. Everyone leaves active duty at some point, and most will need (or want) a civilian job. We want to help you have a successful transition to civilian life and civilian employment.

It's never too early to start thinking about your long-term goals and taking steps, even small ones, to achieve them.

While in the Army, you will learn valuable skills. Strive to be the best in your specialty. One of the reasons veterans sometimes have trouble finding jobs is that they have trouble explaining their military experience in terms that are meaningful to civilian employers.

One of the best ways to do that is by earning a *credential*. A credential is government *license* (usually state governments) or a *certification* from a non-government credentialing agency.

Commercial truck driver's licenses and medical licenses are examples of government-issued credentials.

Non-government credentialing agencies that offer certifications include the National Institute for Automotive Service Excellence, the American Culinary Federation, and the American Welding Society.

You can learn about credentials related to your MOS on the website "Army Credentialing Opportunities On-line at https://www.cool.army.mil/ (or do a search under "Army COOL"). You will learn more about credentialing in your military training and from the leaders in your unit of assignment.

Soldiers in some fields are *required* to earn credentials, such as an FAA license for Air Traffic Controllers, but for most Soldiers, credentialing programs are voluntary.

You may work on a credential on your own, or you might have the opportunity to participate in an Army sponsored credentialing program.

Most of these programs are offered to students in Army schools. When you go to an Army School, you might be asked if you want to volunteer to take a credentialing exam. The Army might give you study material, including web-based training. They might pay your fees and make arrangements for you to take the exam. We encourage you to take advantage of these programs, take them seriously, and study.

You might earn a valuable credential that will someday make your job application stand out.

The Army believes that studying for a credential in your field makes you a more well-rounded Soldier, and it is one sign that you are a true professional in your military specialty.

It is difficult to provide general information about credentials, because there is so much variety among military specialties and among credentials and credentialing agencies.

Some military specialties (for example, Motor Transport Operators, Wheeled Vehicle Mechanics, Food Service Specialists, and many others) closely match civilian jobs. Other valuable military specialties, such as Infantrymen and Armor Crew Members, do not match civilian jobs.

If you are in a specialty that does not closely match a civilian job and does not have a lot of credentialing opportunities, there are several things you can do. Some of these are good ideas for all Soldiers:

- In the words of the Chief of Staff of the Army, the best credential is often a college degree. When you finish your Initial Military Training, talk the Career Counselor in your unit and to an Education Counselor, they can advise you about continuing your education.

- Remember that you are still learning life skills that will be valuable to an employer. Army Veterans tend to be reliable, hard-working, goal-oriented, "team players" and drug-free. As a future Non-Commissioned Officer (sergeant), you will learn leadership, effective communication, how to train others, and how to supervise a job site.
- Even if your "main job" doesn't match a civilian job, take advantage of any opportunities that come your way to learn new skills, for example, computer skills and operating and maintaining different types of equipment.
- Keep checking! The Army is developing new credentialing opportunities.

Tips and Precautions: One of the reasons that some credentials are so valuable is that they are hard to get. If you sign up for a credentialing exam, study!

- If you did your best, don't be discouraged if you don't pass on the first try. Remember everything you learned by studying to take the exam, and consider trying again.
- If you choose a credential to work on, be sure that the credential is the right one for you. Before you spend your money or use up some of your military benefits, make sure that the credential is offered

by a reputable agency and is known and valued by employers.
- Many credentials have re-certification requirements or continuing education requirements. Know what they are.
- Army COOL, Army Career Tracker, and credentialing agency websites contain a wealth of information. Talk to your instructors and leaders, your unit Career Counselor and education counselors. Ask questions!

A-8. Information websites for family members

The Army recognizes the important role that spouses and Family members play in supporting Soldiers and in keeping our Army communities strong.

Each Army installation has its own website that is full of useful information for your Family and can be found by searching for the name of the installation on the internet.

Be sure to look for the official site indicated by the ending "army.mil" in the web address. We have provided you with a few useful websites to vital information sources throughout this Blue Book and additional sources are located below.

It is extremely important to you and the Army that we link your Family members with resources to help integrate them into the Army lifestyle.

Use these websites and the others embedded in this book as you progress through your career from BCT to your first unit of assignment.

They will provide a wide variety of information to your Family and help them progress with you throughout your Army career.

- Start here with the "Army Family and New Spouse Orientation" video.
  http://vimeo.com/9936630

- My Army One-Source answers hundreds of Family-related questions.
  http://www.myarmyonesource.com

- Army Knowledge On-Line (AKO) will allow you to sponsor your spouse with an AKO account similar to yours.
  https://www.us.army.mil

- Commanding General for Initial Military Training Knowledge Center requires an AKO account to log-in and provides information about your training and resources available to you and your Family.

https://www.us.army.mil/suite/page/630102

- Civilian Personnel On-line is where your spouse can look for and apply for a job with the Army at any Army installation and the Army gives spouses an employment preference.
  https://www.usajobs.gov/

- Family members new to Army life can find answers to their questions regarding Army benefits. http://myarmybenefits.us.army.mil

- Contact the Red Cross to notify a Soldier of a Family emergency and/or search for your local Red Cross representative. www.redcross.org

- The official TRICARE web site is where you and your Family members can find information on military healthcare coverage.
  www.tricare.mil

- Visit the Dental Program online for local dentists in your area and information regarding dental care.
  www.tricare.mil/dental/TDP.aspx

- Your LES and other pay information can be obtained from the official MyPay Homepage.
  https://mypay.dfas.mil/

- Army COOL (Credentialing Opportunities On-Line). https://www.cool.army.mil/

- Army Career Tracker: https://actnow.army.mil/

- Improved Outer Tactical Vest (IOTV)
  https://www.youtube.com/watch?v=1CtmLG45k_A&feature=youtu.be

Appendix B – Manual of Applied Performance Skills (MAPS)

Manual of Applied Performance Skills (MAPS)

Your MAPS to Navigate Basic Combat Training

Contents

Content	Page #
I. Main Module - First Hour	
The Mental Fitness Continuum	4
Resilience Skills to Help Throughout BCT	6
Adjust Your Thoughts	8
Restructure Your Thoughts	9
Acceptance	10
Self-Talk	10
II. Main Module - Second Hour	
Manage Your Emotions & Reactions	11
Optimism & Hunt the Good Stuff	11
Grounding	12
Achieve Your Goals	12
Goal Setting	13
Goals Setting Examples and Practice	14-18
Hunt the Good Stuff Journal	19-29
III. Mini-Modules:	
Attention Control and Confidence	30-38
Deliberate Breathing	39-48
Imagery and Routines	49-56
IV. Notes Pages	57-68

Main Module

How to Use Your MAPS Booklet

Just like a real map gets you where you need to go, this MAPS booklet is designed to help you get your mind where it needs to go in order to maximize your performance throughout Basic Combat Training.

You're encouraged to use this booklet to help you prepare for and reflect back on key BCT / OSUT events as a sort of training log — something 90% of US Olympic athletes report using to help them strengthen their minds and bodies when they are training.

> "We have to take our Soldiers from the time they come into the Army and build resiliency within them all the way until the time they get out." -Gen. John F. Campbell, Vice Chief of Staff of the Army

The Mental Fitness Continuum

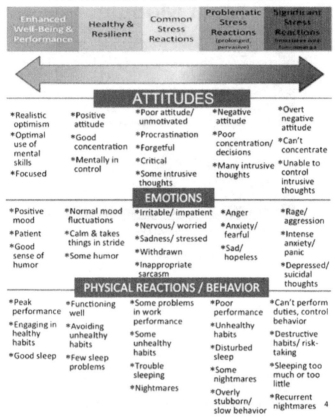

Enhanced Well-Being & Performance	Healthy & Resilient	Common Stress Reactions	Problematic Stress Reactions (prolonged, pervasive)	Significant Stress Reactions
ATTITUDES				
*Realistic optimism *Optimal use of mental skills *Focused	*Positive attitude *Good concentration *Mentally in control	*Poor attitude/ unmotivated *Procrastination *Forgetful *Critical *Some intrusive thoughts	*Negative attitude *Poor concentration/ decisions *Many intrusive thoughts	*Overt negative attitude *Can't concentrate *Unable to control intrusive thoughts
EMOTIONS				
*Positive mood *Patient *Good sense of humor	*Normal mood fluctuations *Calm & takes things in stride *Some humor	*Irritable/ impatient *Nervous/ worried *Sadness/ stressed *Withdrawn *Inappropriate sarcasm	*Anger *Anxiety/ fearful *Sad/ hopeless	*Rage/ aggression *Intense anxiety/ panic *Depressed/ suicidal thoughts
PHYSICAL REACTIONS / BEHAVIOR				
*Peak performance *Engaging in healthy habits *Good sleep	*Functioning well *Avoiding unhealthy habits *Few sleep problems	*Some problems in work performance *Some unhealthy habits *Trouble sleeping *Nightmares	*Poor performance *Unhealthy habits *Disturbed sleep *Some nightmares *Overly stubborn/ slow behavior	*Can't perform duties, control behavior *Destructive habits/ risk-taking *Sleeping too much or too little *Recurrent nightmares

Resilience

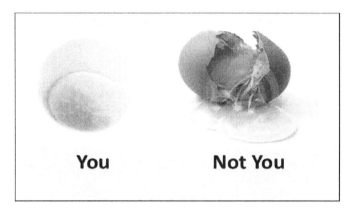

- **Resilience** is the ability to withstand, recover, grow, and thrive in the face of stressors and changing demands.
- Instead of breaking when faced with a tough situation, resilient Soldiers bounce back like a tennis ball.
- Stuff happens and BCT / OSUT is going to be tough, but you can control how you respond.
- It's not just the fortunate few who can be resilient – these are skills anyone can learn.
- That's why you are receiving this training. It's designed to develop resilient Soldiers.

Resilience Skills You Will Learn

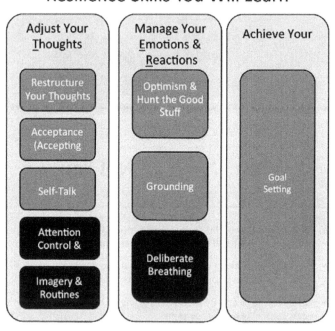

Note: The skills in the dark green boxes are those you will learn in mini-modules later on in BCT / OSUT.

Each of these skills is something that you can do by yourself in just a few minutes to help you deal with the stressful things happening to and around you, especially situations and events that you cannot control.

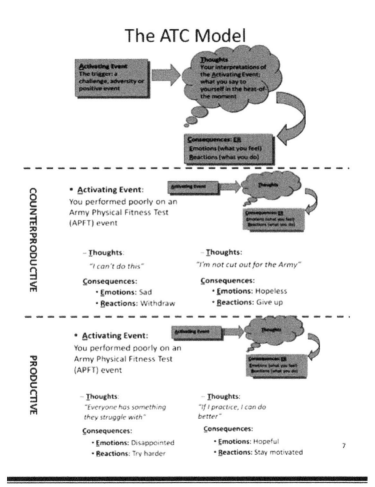

Adjust Your Thoughts

Is there a need to adjust your Thoughts?

- As a result of a situation or event, did you receive a desirable outcome?
    - **Yes**: No action needed
    - **No**: Identify what is controllable and uncontrollable
- When you need to adjust your Thoughts
    - **Step 1:** For the parts of the situation or event that can be changed (controlled), take action to change those parts.

        Physically prepare and move on to the next task

    - **Step 2**: For the parts of the situation or event that you can't control, your Initial Thoughts may need to be adjusted.

        Adjust the Thoughts you had initially

---

3 Ways to Adjust Your Thoughts

1) Restructuring Thoughts
2) Acceptance
3) Self-Talk

Restructure Your Thoughts

- <u>Restructure Your Thoughts</u>: Thinking about the event from a different perspective is a resilience strategy

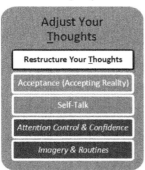

- Examples of when it would be helpful
    - When you've performed poorly and are hard on yourself
    - When battle buddies are being hard on themselves

Non-Optimal Thoughts	Restructured Thoughts
"I'm an idiot and let my buddies down."	"I won't do that again; I've learned my lesson."
"I'm not going to make it through BCT / OSUT."	"If that's the worst thing I do here, I'm doing pretty well."
"They're all going to hate me."	"Everyone messes up; it's not the end of the world."
"I always screw up."	"I messed up this one task in this one way; I didn't mess up everything."

- Remember your <u>T</u>houghts drive your <u>C</u>onsequences

Manage Your Emotions & Reactions
Optimism & Hunt the Good Stuff

- Optimism: hopefulness and confidence about the future or the successful outcome of something
- Hunt the Good Stuff (HTGS): skill that builds optimism by finding and reflecting on the good things is a resilience strategy

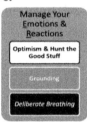

- Examples of when it would be helpful
    - At the end of the day
    - With battle buddies

- **Optimism is about:**
    - Remaining realistic
    - Identifying what's controllable
    - Maintaining hope
    - Having confidence in yourself and your team
- **Hunt the Good Stuff** leads to Optimism and Optimism can result in:
    - Better health, better sleep, feeling calm
    - Lower depression and greater life satisfaction
    - More optimal performance
    - Better relationships

"Perpetual optimism is a force multiplier." -GEN (Ret.) Colin Powell

Grounding

- Grounding: a resilience skill used to regain your focus, and control your energy levels

- Examples of when it would be helpful
  - When your mind is wandering away from the task at hand
  - When taught to a battle buddy who is anxious or nervous and needs to calm down
- Grounding helps bring your focus back to the present by controlling your arousal and counteracting negative effects of adrenaline
- Do 3x3 exercise to ground — Identify 3 things you can:
  - See
  - Hear
  - Feel (physically)

Achieve Your Goals
Goal Setting

- Goal Setting: A resilience skill to help you identify your goals and develop a plan to achieve them
- Examples of when it would be helpful
  - When you start something new (such as school, the Army)
  - When you need to train for a major physical event (such as the APFT)

Goal Setting

- Pick your goal
- Break your big goal down into at least 2 short-term goals (daily or weekly)
  - Think about areas where you need to improve
  - Get help from a battle buddy
  - Connect to your goal every day
- Write 2-3 SMART action statements for each sub-goal
  - **S**pecific
  - **M**easurable
  - **A**ction-Focused
  - **R**elevant
  - **T**ime-Bound
- Write one effective Self-Talk sentence for each of your sub-goals to encourage yourself

Big Goal	270 on APFT
Short-Term Goal: (3-4 to help you achieve your big goal)	I will eat more nutritious meals in the DFAC until the final APFT.

SMART = Specific, Measurable, Action-Focused, Realistic, Time-Bound (3-4 per short-term goal)	SMART Action 1:	I drink at least 80 ounces of water a day.
	SMART Action 2:	I eat 60% clean carbs, 30% healthy fat, and 10% lean protein a day.
	SMART Action 3:	I drink no more than one sports drink a day.
Self-Talk Statement: (One to stay motivated and energized)		At meal times, I tell myself that I expect great things out of my body so I put only great things in my body.

(See next pages for examples and space to create your own Goal Setting plans.)

GOAL Setting Example #1

Goal	270 on APFT
Short-Term Goal A: Help you achieve the big goal (at least 3)	I will eat more nutritious meals and snacks in the next four weeks than I did the last four weeks
SMART Action 1:	I drink no less than 80 ounces of water a day
SMART Action 2:	I eat 60% clean carbs, 30% healthy fat, and 10% lean protein every day
SMART Action 3:	I drink no more than one sports drink a day
Self-Talk: (1 per short-term goal)	At meal times, I tell myself that I expect great things out of my body so I put only great things in my body
Short-Term Goal B: Help you achieve the big goal (at least 3)	I will reduce my run time by 30 seconds
SMART Action 1:	I run at least 3 miles twice a week
SMART Action 2:	I go for a longer run of more than 3 miles every other weekend
SMART Action 3:	I ice my knees after every run that's longer than a mile
Self-Talk: (1 per short-term goal)	When I get tired of running, I remind myself that I get stronger and more prepared with each step
Short-Term Goal C: Help you achieve the big goal (at least 3)	I will improve my attitude and believe in myself
SMART Action 1:	I practice confident Self-Talk deliberately at least 5 times a day
SMART Action 2:	I pay attention to my Self-Talk and make sure it's helping me accomplish my goals
SMART Action 3:	I remain optimistic by Hunting the Good Stuff every night before bed
Self-Talk: (1 per short-term goal)	Before bed, I remind myself that I am prepared, I am confident, and I am capable

Goal Setting Example #2

Goal	Successfully negotiate the LandNav course within the allotted time
Short-Term Goal A:	I will increase my comfort in the basic use of a military map by 2 weeks prior to the course
SMART Action 1:	I identify map marginal info on 2 military maps each night
SMART Action 2:	I determine the scale of the map and corresponding protractor grid scale and placement for 2 maps each night
SMART Action 3:	I convert grid north to magnetic north and reverse on 2 maps each night
Self-Talk:	I tell myself I'm not alone, my battle buddy is part of my team. I have my battle buddy's back and my battle buddy has mine
Short-Term Goal B:	I will become proficient in plotting points and measuring distances on a military map 2 weeks prior to the course
SMART Action 1:	I ID 6 digit grid coordinates for 2 start and end points on a map each night with a battle buddy
SMART Action 2:	I measure 2 straight and 2 curved line distances on a map each night with a battle buddy
SMART Action 3:	I orient the map I am working with to the ground each night until the LandNav course
Self-Talk:	I tell myself that slow is smooth, smooth is fast. The more accurate I am, the less time I will need
Short-Term Goal C:	I will increase my personal Land Navigation confidence by 1 week prior to the course
SMART Action 1:	I pace count known distances in various terrain while walking and running at locations available in the company area each night
SMART Action 2:	I practice Deliberate Breathing for 5 minutes before I practice my LandNav skills each night and throughout my practice time
SMART Action 3:	I imagine myself successfully completing the LandNav course for 10 minutes before I go to sleep each night
Self-Talk:	I tell myself I've practiced with my battle buddies over and over so I'm ready. I trust my training.

Goal Setting Practice—APFT

Goal

Short-Term Goal A:

    SMART Action 1:

    SMART Action 2:

    SMART Action 3:

Self-Talk:

Short-Term Goal B:

    SMART Action 1:

    SMART Action 2:

    SMART Action 3:

Self-Talk:

Short-Term Goal C:

    SMART Action 1:

    SMART Action 2:

    SMART Action 3:

Self-Talk:

Goal Setting Practice—BCT / OSUT

Goal

Short-Term Goal A:

SMART Action 1:

SMART Action 2:

SMART Action 3:

Self-Talk:

Short-Term Goal B:

SMART Action 1:

SMART Action 2:

SMART Action 3:

Self-Talk:

Short-Term Goal C:

SMART Action 1:

SMART Action 2:

SMART Action 3:

Self-Talk:

Goal Setting Practice—Army Career

Goal

Short-Term Goal A:

    SMART Action 1:

    SMART Action 2:

    SMART Action 3:

Self-Talk:

Short-Term Goal B:

    SMART Action 1:

    SMART Action 2:

    SMART Action 3:

Self-Talk:

Short-Term Goal C:

    SMART Action 1:

    SMART Action 2:

    SMART Action 3:

Self-Talk:

Hunt the Good Stuff Journal

Instructions: To Hunt the Good Stuff, record three good things each day

- Next to each positive event you list, write a reflection (at least one sentence) about ONE of these things:
  - Why this good thing happened
  - What this good thing means to you
  - What you can do tomorrow to enable more of this good thing
  - What ways you or others contributed to this good thing

"A pessimist is one who makes difficulties of his opportunities and an optimist is one who makes opportunities of his difficulties." -Harry S. Truman

Hunt the Good Stuff Practice

Date: _____

Good Stuff (Positive Event)	Reflection

Hunt the Good Stuff Practice

Date: _____

Good Stuff (Positive Event)	Reflection

Hunt the Good Stuff Practice

Date: _____

Good Stuff (Positive Event)	Reflection

Mini-Module: Attention Control and Confidence

Attention Control and Confidence Overview

- What is it?
    - Attention control means paying attention to the most important things around you
    - Building confidence helps you improve your performance by reducing doubt that can distract you
- How does it work?
    - Focus on **W**hat's **I**mportant **N**ow
    - Build confidence in 4 ways

Attention is a Limited Resource

- Research shows that people using cell phones while driving are:
    - 2x more likely to miss traffic signals
    - When they do see the traffic signal, reaction time is slower
- Perform your best by focusing your limited attention on the task at hand

Please, No Cell Phone Use While Driving

"If there is a secret for greater self-control, the science points to one thing: the power of paying attention." -Kelly McGonigal, *The Willpower Instinct: How Self-Control Works, Why It Matters, and What You Can Do to Get More of It*

WIN

- To focus your attention on the task, think WIN
  - **W**hat's
  - **I**mportant
  - **N**ow

- For example, think about climbing the cargo net rather than how you got off to a slow start
- Focus on what you can do and/or control now

Confidence

- **Confidence**: Degree of certainty about your ability to execute action to produce an outcome
- 4 sources of confidence
  1. Personal experience
  2. Physical state
  3. Observing others
  4. Self-Talk

Adjust Your Thoughts
- Restructure Your Thoughts
- Acceptance (Accepting Reality)
- Self-Talk
- Attention Control & Confidence
- Imagery & Routines

"When you have confidence, you can have a lot of fun. And when you have fun, you can do amazing things." -Joe Namath

Personal Experience

- **Past experience** can help you feel confident
    - Success builds enthusiasm, optimism
    - Failure builds competence, helps you make adjustments

> What have you already accomplished in BCT / OSUT and/or in your life up to this point that might help you feel confident in your ability to complete BCT / OSUT?

Physical State

- How you feel when you're tired and hungry versus well-rested, prime physical condition
- **Feeling physically ready** helps you feel confident
- Anxiety can also reduce confidence, but you can fight it with Deliberate Breathing *(or deep breathing if you haven't learned about Deliberate Breathing yet)*

> How do you want to physically feel before important BCT / OSUT events?

Notes:

Observing Others

- Gain confidence by **observing someone else's performance**, so watch other people while you wait for your turn
- When you see someone who has **similar abilities to you**:
    - Gain confidence when they succeed
    - Get information about ways to adjust and perform better if they fail

---

Record an example of when you felt more confident after watching someone else do something:

Self-Talk

- Use **Self-Talk to focus on the task** and help you rely on your training for optimal performance
    - For example, you can say to yourself:
        - *"I can do this"*
        - *"I am trained for this"*
- Use Productive Self-Talk to walk yourself through the event, then walk your buddy through it

---

Record some effective Self-Talk statements you might use to walk yourself through the Confidence Obstacle Course:

Fearful Thinking and Self-Talk

I'm not strong enough for this!

Obviously, I'm supposed to become Tarzan to get through this!

It would be easier to scale the Empire State Building!

Record some fearful Thoughts you might be having about the major event:

More Effective Thoughts & Self-Talk

The wall hanger is just like the monkey bars!

Companies pay lots of money for teambuilding courses like this!

People do this all the time for the Warrior Dash—and they LOVE it!

Record some more effective, optimal Thoughts about the major event or Productive Self-Talk you could use to help you get through it:

Attention Control and Confidence in Review

- Attention is limited so you have to focus on **WIN**
- Build confidence through:
  - **Personal experience**
  - **Physical state**
  - **Observing others**
  - **Self-talk**
- Use productive, effective Self-Talk to replace fearful thoughts and coach yourself and your buddy through key events

Mini-Module: Deliberate Breathing

Notes:

Deep Survival & Deliberate Breathing

- Deliberate Breathing helps you build, access "Composure Under Fire"

- **Composure under fire** or **inner cool** refers to a cool, calm, and confident attitude that helped people survive traumatic situations (according to Gonzales)

- What is **Deliberate Breathing**?
    - A way to gain physical, mental, and emotional control under extreme stress, if practiced and rehearsed in advance
    - A way to channel Inner Cool
        - Not *just* deep breathing
        - Use before key BCT / OSUT events (like CBRN Chamber)

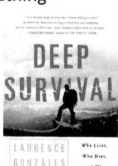

Adjust Your Emotions & Reactions

Optimism & Hunt the Good Stuff

Grounding

Deliberate Breathing

"$*#@ does just happen sometimes... There are things you can't control, so you'd better know how you're going to react to them... But there are also the things you can control, and you'd better be controlling them all the time." -Laurence Gonzales, *Deep Survival*

Deliberate Breathing Overview

- **Composure under fire** may be learned
    - Train it and build it by using Deliberate Breathing
- How does **Deliberate Breathing** work?
    - Combines **physical, mental, and emotional control**
    - Focuses Thoughts in order to avoid "paralysis by analysis"
    - Directs Thoughts to what you need to focus on in the moment

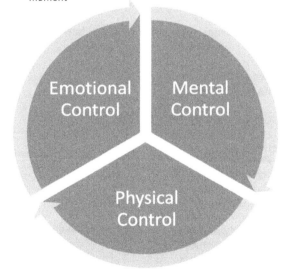

Benefits of Deliberate Breathing

Scientifically-Supported Benefits	Targets of Opportunity
Improves memory and recall	CBRN Chamber, CLS written exam, Warrior basic knowledge
Improves decision making and mental agility	CBRN Chamber, Confidence Obstacle Course (COC), FTX
Improves alertness, focus, and concentration	CBRN Chamber and everything else
Improves coordination on fine motor tasks	RM
Improves recovery following gross motor tasks *(like crawling or running)*	APFT, COC
Improves emotional control during stressful situations	COC, RM
Reduces fatigue during longer operations	APFT, COC, Field Marches, FTX

Physical Control

- Get it by using a **"tactical pause"**
- Embrace the phrase **"Stop, Unlock, and Breathe"**

  - **Stop**—sit still, uncross legs and arms to promote circulation
  - **Unlock**—let go of unnecessary muscle tension and physical stress
  - **Breathe**—breathe slow, low, and deep
    - **"5-5 cadence"** - five-count inhale and five-count exhale

Mental Control

- **Mental control**—quiet the analytical mind, focus on what's happening now (the feel and rhythm of your breath)

Emotional Control

- **Emotional control**— "park" your counterproductive emotions in a parking lot nearby

"When you own your breath, nobody can steal your peace." -Author Unknown

Deliberate Breathing Practice

- Deliberate Breathing focused on a **5-second cadence**
- Deliberate Breathing focused on a **physical sensation**
- Deliberate Breathing focused on a **relaxation cue**
- Deliberate Breathing focused on a **positive emotion**

Record any notes you have about practicing Deliberate Breathing (such as the cues you used or which method you liked best):

Personal After Action Review (PAAR): Confidence Builders

- After you complete the major event, record at least 3 personal successes from the event (**Confidence Builders**)

| 1 | *I followed every one of Drill Sergeant's coaching commands and responded with a confident voice* |

2

3

4

PAAR: Competence Builders

- Now add up to 3 corrections and/or improvements to make in order to get better (**Competence Builders**)

1	*Next time, I will use Deliberate Breathing more consistently*
2	
3	
4	

PAAR: Recovery Plan

- Record how you will recover following this event

| 1 | *I will take a minute or two in between events and 5 minutes before bed to "Stop, Unlock, and Breathe"* |

2

> "Mentally tough athletes are really good at making adjustments and doing them quickly. They look for a lesson in it, and if there is none, they move on."
> -Chris Carr, sports psychologist who works with U.S. Olympic teams

Deliberate Breathing in Review

- **Practice Deliberate Breathing BEFORE** challenges to build and access your Composure Under Fire
- Choose from three different topics to think about during Deliberate Breathing
    - 5-second cadence
    - Physical sensation
    - Relaxation cue
    - Positive emotion

Emotional Control
- Park your Emotions on the side

Physical Control
- "Stop, Unlock, & Breathe"
- 5-5 cadence

Mental Control
- Quiet your mind
- Focus on task at hand

Mini-Module:
Imagery and Routines

Imagery and Routines Overview

- What is it?
  - **Imagery**: Purposeful daydreaming or visualization to help you get ready for an event
  - **Routines**: Standard procedures
- How does it work?
  - Use Imagery to develop a routine
  - **Imagery**
    - Brain can't tell the difference between reality and an imagined event so your body responds like the event is real
    - Improves "muscle memory," strengthens the mental blueprint of skills
  - **Routines**: Actions done so often in a particular order to prepare you mentally and physically to perform so that you can focus on WIN

Adjust Your Thoughts
- Acceptance (Accepting Reality)
- Restructure Your Thoughts
- Self-Talk
- Attention Control & Confidence
- Imagery & Routines

Using Mental Imagery

- Elite athletes, very successful people report using Imagery
  - Michael Phelps
  - Jim Thorpe
- Mental imagery + physical practice are best
  - Mental Imagery is better than nothing
- Science shows highly skilled individuals use Imagery more than less-skilled people

"He's the best I've ever seen and maybe the best ever in terms of visualization. He will see exactly the perfect race. He'll see it like he is in the stands and he'll see it like he's in the water."
-Bob Bowman, coach of Olympic swimmer Michael Phelps

Using a Routine

- You already use routines, but now you will consciously create one for RM
- Firing routines improve performance because they:
  - Help you focus on how you shoot, not the results
  - Keep your mind on the present mission
- To develop an effective firing routine:
  - Shoot and think the same way every time
  - Keep your Thoughts simple
  - Practice and rehearse it often

Gladiator Routines

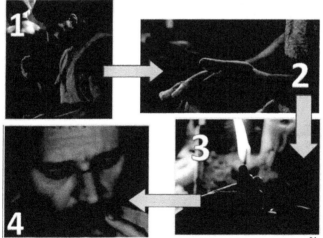

"Ready, Set, Go"

TEA
Thoughts
Energy
Attention

"Ready" Your Thoughts

- Use "**ready**" as cue word when preparing for event
- Thoughts should be productive **Self-Talk** (like Self-Talk involved in Goal Setting)
- Keep it simple
- Use **Imagery** to see your success

Productive Self-Talk Statement:
See the target, hit the target!

Productive Self-Talk Statement Ideas:

"**Set**" Your **E**nergy

- Just before the event, **embrace your nervousness**
    - Accept and thank your body for the extra adrenaline
- Be comfortable being uncomfortable
- **Deliberate Breathing**
    - "Stop, Unlock, and Breathe"
- Include this stage in your Imagery

Energy Cue:

Alert and Focused

Energy Cue Ideas:

Focus <u>A</u>ttention and Let "Go"

- When it's time for the event, focus attention where you need it, on **the WIN that helps you fire your weapon**
- Then let **"Go" and fire with your eyes and not your brain**

Attention to WIN:
Breathe, Relax, Aim, or Squeeze

Attention to your WIN:

Imagery and Routines in Review

- Before the Event: "**Ready**" Your T̲houghts
    - Use productive Self-Talk
    - Use Imagery to visualize all three stages
    - Keep it simple
- Just Before the Event: "**Set**" Your E̲nergy
    - Embrace nervousness
    - Be comfortable being uncomfortable
    - Deliberate Breathing
- During the Event: Focus A̲ttention and "**Go**"
    - Focus on your WIN to help you fire your weapon
    - Fire with your eyes, not your brain

"Excellence is an art won by training and habituation.... We are what we repeatedly do. Excellence, then, is not an act but a habit." -Aristotle

Appendix C – Soldier's Notes

Glossary

ACE	Ask, Care, Escort
ACT	Army Career Tracker
ACU	Army Combat Uniform
AER	Army Emergency Relief
AIT	advanced individual training
APFT	Army Physical Fitness Test
APFU	Army Physical Fitness Uniform
AR	Army Regulation
ARNG	Army National Guard
ASU	Army Service Uniform
BCAC	Beneficiary Counseling and Assistance Coordinator
BCT	Basic Combat Training
DEERS	Defense Enrollment Eligibility Reporting System
EO	Equal Opportunity
FM	Field Manual
FTX	Field Training Exercise
ID	Identification
IET	Initial Entry Training
LDRSHIP	Loyalty, Duty, Respect, Selfless Service, Honor, Integrity, and Personal Courage
LES	Leave and Earning Statement
MAPS	Manual of Applied Performance Skills
MOS	Military Occupational Specialty

NCO	Noncommissioned Officer
OPAT	Occupational Physical Assessment Test
OSUT	One Station Unit Training
SARC	Sexual Assault Response Coordinator
SFL	Soldier for Life
SGLI	Service Member's Group Life Insurance
SHARP	Sexual Harassment/Assault Response and Prevention
STX	Situational Training Exercise
TASP	Total Army Sponsorship Program
TRICARE	Tri-service Health Care
UCMJ	Uniform Code of Military Justice
USAR	United States Army Reserve
VA	Victim Advocate
WTBDs	Warrior Tasks and Battle Drills

Army Definitions

A

Advanced Individual Training - a training course where Soldiers learn skills in a specific military occupational specialty

AIT Platoon Sergeant- a highly educated AIT Non-Commissioned Officer who supervises, manages Soldiers and trains skills in a specific military occupational specialty

Army Values- values that characterize the Army's professionalism and culture, and describe the ethical standards expected of all Soldiers

Army Emergency Relief- A private nonprofit organization incorporated in 1942 by the Secretary of War and the Army Chief of Staff.

Army Ethics- The evolving set of laws, values, and beliefs, embedded within the Army culture of trust that motivates and guides the conduct of Army professionals bound together in common moral purpose.

Army Profession- A member of the Army Profession who meets the Army's certification criteria of competence, character, and commitment.

B

Base- the element around which a movement is planned or regulated

Basic Combat Training- a training course that transforms civilians into Soldiers

Buddy Team- two Soldiers in the same unit who look after each other at all times

Bugle Call- the musical signal that announces scheduled and certain non-scheduled events on an Army installation

C

Cadence- a uniform rhythm or number of steps or counts per minute

Chaplain- a spiritual support officer to every Soldier

Code of Conduct- guidance on how a Soldier must conduct him or herself if captured by the enemy

Commissioned Officer- an officer who is commissioned into the U.S. Army; leaders with the authority to command Soldiers

Conditioning Drill- a strength and mobility activity that helps Soldiers improve their functional strength, postural alignment, and body mechanics as the exercises relate to the quality performance of Warrior Tasks and Battle Drills

D

Distance- the space between elements that are one behind the other; the distance between individuals is an arm's length, plus 6 inches, or approximately 36 inches measured from the chest of one Soldier to the back of the Soldier immediately to his front

Double Time- a cadence of 180 counts (steps per minute)

Drill Command- an oral order given by a commander or leader, usually in two parts; the preparatory command states the movement to be carried out and gets you ready to execute the order; the command of execution tells when the movement is to be carried out

Drill Sergeant- a highly educated, qualified noncommissioned officer and the primary instructor in IET who transform civilians into Soldiers

Duty- to fulfill your obligations

E

Element- an individual, squad, section, platoon, company, or larger unit formed as part of the next higher unit

Equal Opportunity- equal treatment for military personnel, and civilian employees without regard to race, color, religion, gender, or national origin

F

File- a column that has a front of one element

Formal Complaint- an EO complaint in which a Soldier, Family member, or DA civilian files in writing and swears to the accuracy of the information

Formation- an arrangement of the unit's elements in a prescribed manner such as a line formation in which the elements are side-by-side, and column formation in which the elements are one behind the other

Fraternization- personal relationships between officer and enlisted personnel regardless of their service; same-gender relationships; relationships between permanent party members and IET Soldiers; relationships between IET Soldiers; violations punishable under UCMJ

Front- a space from one side to the other side of a formation, and includes the right and left elements

G

General Courts-Martial- a courts-martial that consists of a military judge and not less than five panel members when required; held for serious offenses

Guide- the person responsible for maintaining the prescribed direction and rate of march

H

Head- a column's leading element

Honor- to live up to the Army Values

I

Informal Complaint- any EO complaint that a Soldier, Family member or DA civilian does not wish to file in writing

Integrity- to do what is right, legally and morally

Interval- the space between side-by-side elements

L

Leave and Earnings Statement- a detailed pay statement issued at the end of each month to military service members, retirees, and DA civilians; statement contains nine sections related to military earnings and leave

Loyalty- to bear true faith and allegiance to the U.S. Constitution, the Army, your unit, and other Soldiers

M

Marksmanship Badge- a badge awarded to individuals who qualify, because they have demonstrated some special proficiency or skill; a badge worn to indicate the individual's prowess with specific weapons, pistols, and/or rifles and during specified competitions, matches, or practice exercises

Medal- Commemorative, campaign, and service medals are issued to Soldiers who take part in particular campaigns or periods of service for which a medal is authorized

Medal of Honor- the highest and most rarely awarded decoration conferred by the U.S. The medal is awarded for conspicuous gallantry and intrepidity at the risk of his or her life above and beyond the call of duty while engaged in an action against an enemy of the U.S.

Military Time- a time table based on the 24-hour clock system

N

Noncommissioned Officer (NCO) - a senior enlisted technical expert, combat leader, mentor, and primary advisor to the commander

O

Oath of Enlistment- the oath Soldiers make to officially enlist into the U. S. Army; the oath to support and defend the United States of America and the U.S. Constitution

One-Station-Unit-Training (OSUT) - basic combat training and advanced individual training combined into one course

Occupational Physical Assessment Test (OPAT) – Test to assess physical ability to perform certain requirements in order to receive training for a specific occupation in the Army.

P

Personal Courage- to face and overcome fear, danger or adversity (physical or moral)

Post- the correct place for an officer or NCO to stand in a prescribed formation

Purple Heart- a medal awarded to persons serving in any capacity as a member of the Armed Forces who are killed or wounded (requiring treatment by a medical officer) in any action against enemies of the U.S.

Q

Quick Time- a cadence of 120 counts (steps per minute)

R

Rank- a line that is only one element in depth
Respect- to treat people as they should be treated
Restricted Reporting- A reporting option that allows military sexual assault victims to confidentially disclose the assault to a SARC, VA, or Health Care Provider and receive medical treatment, including emergency care, counseling, and assignment of a SARC and VA, without triggering an official investigation. The victim's report provided to healthcare SARCs, or VAs will NOT be reported to law enforcement or to the command to initiate the official investigative process unless the victim consents. Only a SARC, SAPR VA, or healthcare personnel may receive a Restricted Report. A Victim can also speak to a Chaplain without triggering an official investigation however, Chaplains cannot initiate a restricted report.
Risk Management- a decision-making process used to identify and eliminate or reduce risks associated with *all* hazards that have the potential to injure or kill personnel, damage or destroy equipment, or otherwise impact mission effectiveness

S

Sexual Assault Response Coordinator (SARC) - The SARC is the single point of contact within an organization or installation that oversees sexual assault awareness, prevention, and response training;

coordinates medical treatment, including emergency care, for victims of sexual assault; and tracks the services provided to a victim of sexual assault from the initial report through final disposition and resolution. The SARC is responsible for ensuring that victims of sexual assault receive appropriate and responsive care. Upon notification of a sexual assault and after receiving consent from the victim, the SARC will assign a VA to assist the victim. SARCs supervise VAs, but are authorized to perform VA duties if required.

Selfless Service- to put the welfare of the Nation, the Army, and your subordinates before your own

Service Member's Group Life Insurance (SGLI) - military life insurance

Sexual Assault- a crime defined as intentional sexual contact, characterized by use of force, physical threat, or abuse of authority or when victim does not or cannot consent. "Consent" will not be deemed or construed to mean the failure by the victim to offer physical resistance. Consent is not given when a person uses force, threat of force, or coercion or when the victim is asleep, incapacitated, or unconscious.

Sexual Contact- Touching or causing another person to touch, either directly or through clothing either genitalia, anus, groin, breast, inner thigh or buttocks with an intent to abuse, humiliate or degrade any person; or touching or causing another person to touch any body part of that person, either directly or through clothing if done with an intent to arouse/gratify sexual desire.

Sexual Harassment- a form of gender discrimination that involves unwelcome sexual advances, requests for sexual favors, and other verbal, or physical conduct of a sexual nature

Soldier- a highly dedicated, uniformed member of the U.S. Army who stands ready to defend the United States from its enemies

Soldierization- an extensive five-phase training program in Initial Entry Training

Special Court-Martial- a courts-martial that consists of a military judge and not less than three panel members when required. It is held for relatively serious offenses

Summary Courts-Martial- a court-martial composed of a commissioned officer on active duty with the grade of captain or above. The purpose of the summary court-martial is to make thorough and impartial inquiries into minor offenses and to make sure that justice is done, with the interests of both the government and the accused being safeguarded

T

Thrift Savings Plan- a Federal Government-sponsored retirement savings and investment plan

TRICARE- the Department of Defense's worldwide health care program available to eligible beneficiates from the uniformed services

U

Uniform Code of Military Justice (UCMJ) - the statute that prescribes criminal law for Soldiers

Unrestricted Reporting- A process that an individual uses to disclose, without requesting confidentiality or Restricted Reporting, that he or she is the victim of a sexual assault. Under these circumstances, the victim's report provided to healthcare personnel, the SARC, a SAPR VA, command authorities, or other persons is reported to law enforcement and may be used to initiate the official investigative process.

V

Victim Advocate (VA) - Provides non-clinical crisis intervention, referral, and ongoing non-clinical support to victims. Support includes providing information on available options and resources to victims. The VA, on behalf of the sexual assault victim, provides liaison assistance with other organizations and agencies on victim care matters and reports directly to the SARC when performing victim advocacy duties. VA services are available 24 hours per day, 7 days per week.

W

Warrant Officer- a technical expert, combat leader, trainer, and advisor skilled in a specific technical specialty

Warrior Tasks and Battle Drills (WTBDs) - the critical skills Soldiers are taught in Initial Entry Training; skills Soldiers train on and use throughout their Army career

The United States of America exists because there is a United States Army, which is arguably the best land force the world has ever seen. The U.S. Army is an institution founded on values and a bedrock of trust between it and the American people it serves. The U.S. Army Soldier is professional, disciplined, and reflects the best of our country.

The title of Soldier is never given, it is earned, and what is earned is yours forever. Like the men and women that came before you, from the earliest days of the Revolutionary War to the Mountains of Afghanistan and the deserts of Iraq, the responsibility of defending our nation will be yours. When you graduate Basic Training you will have earned the right to be called Soldier and your name will forever be associated with the greatest Army on Earth.

There are no ex-Soldiers, only Soldiers. Whether you decide to complete one enlistment or make the Army your career, upon completion of honorable service you will have earned the title of Veteran or Retired Soldier but will always be a Soldier for Life. U.S. Army Soldiers, Veterans and Retirees are the strength in our communities and the leaders of our country; you will be that leader.

Once a Soldier, Always a Soldier…a Soldier for Life!
www.soldierforlife.army.mil

Made in the USA
Middletown, DE
14 December 2019